I Want to Be a Gorilla When I'm a Grown-Up

47 Days on the Ohio River

Jonathan Wunrow

Printed in the United States of America

First Printing, 2026

ISBN-13 (Hardcover): 979-8-9988237-3-2
ISBN-13 (Trade Paperback): 979-8-9988237-4-9
ISBN-13 (eBook): 979-8-9988237-5-6

Life is Twisted Press
www.jonwunrow.com

Dedication

This book is dedicated to the many people who have gone out of their way to help this stranger. The people who have offered shelter, shared food, pointed me in the right direction, let me jump in the back of their truck, warned me of danger, or just smiled and gave me a thumbs-up as they passed by. They too are risk takers. I learned from them to offer a smile and reach out my hand to people who just might need both.

Other titles by Jonathan Wunrow
and Life is Twisted Press

High Points: A Climber's Guide to Central America (2012)
Adventure Inward: A Risk Taker's Book of Quotes (2013)
High Points: A Climber's Guide to Central America, Second Edition (2017)
High Points: A Climber's Guide to South America (2018)
Never Stop Walking: A Wales Coast Path Adventure (2021)
Paddling the Mississippi: One Story at a Time (2022)
Me & Sadie, We Got Everything We Need: Stories from Paddling the Tennessee River (2022)
A Walk Across Ireland (2023)
We Are All Nomads: A Bicycle Trip Across Mongolia (2025)

PITTSBURGH RM 0
Allegheny River
Monongahela River
WHEELING RM 260
PARKERSBURG RM 377
MARIETTA RM 399
PORTSMOUTH RM 498
ASHLAND RM 511
HUNTINGTON RM 545
MAYSVILLE RM 640
CINCINNATI RM 663
MADISON RM 681
PARKERSBURG RM 772
OWENSBORO RM 813
EVANSVILLE RM 851
PADUCAH RM 931
CAIRO RM 981
Mississippi River
ILLINOIS
OHIO
INDIANA
KENTUCKY
WEST VIRGINIA
OHIO
THE OHIO RIVER
Total Length: 981 Miles
ILLINOIS
INDIANA
KENTUCKY
OHIO
WEST VIRGINIA
PENNSYLVANIA

"Whatever you can do, or dream you can, begin it.
Boldness has genius, power, and magic in it."
—Goethe

"Let other people go into trances and think about spirituality.
I'd rather concentrate on having something to eat. The here and now."
—Gene Simmons, lead singer of KISS

"An adult is one who has lost the grace, the freshness,
the innocence of the child, who is no longer capable of feeling pure joy,
who makes everything complicated, who spreads suffering everywhere,
who is afraid of being happy, and who, because it is easier to bear,
has gone back to sleep. The wise man is a happy child."
—Arnaud Desjardins

"The point of life is always arrived at in the immediate moment."
—Alan Watts

"It is really difficult to paddle a pumpkin."
—Gary Kristensen, holder of the Guinness World Record for climbing
into a giant, hollowed-out pumpkin and paddling it fifty-five miles
down the Columbia River

Introduction

The other day, I somehow landed on a YouTube video of a guy who was laser focused on growing a gigantic pumpkin, hollowing it out, climbing inside, and attempting to break the distance world record for paddling a pumpkin. The video told the story of Gary Kristensen, who had dreamed of breaking the then–world record of 39.17 miles held by Steve Kueny and set on the Missouri River on October 8, 2023.

On October 12, 2024, Kristensen hauled his 916-pound pumpkin into the Columbia River and climbed in. Twenty-six hours and 54.59 miles later, an exhausted Kristensen climbed out of his pumpkin with the world record. His record-setting adventure was covered by *Outside* magazine, *PBS News Hour*, *Paddling Magazine*, and *USA Today*.

Gary Kristensen had captured the imagination of the country with his unorthodox dream. He had come up with an unconventional—and to be honest, pretty crazy—idea. The kind of idea a small child would have. But Gary set a goal and, relying on his dogged determination, put in the effort to make his dream come true.

A little over a year ago, when I was in the middle of my 981-mile Ohio River thru-paddle, my daughter-in-law Shauna sent me a video of my grandson Rio, who was three years old at the time. In the video, Rio was asked by his mom what he wanted to be when he grew up, and without missing a beat, he replied, "I want to be a gorilla when I'm a grown-up." He was serious.

Rio's unfiltered and honest answer to a question that usually elicits responses like fireman, astronaut, and doctor, has stuck with me ever since.

Why is it that as we get older and grow into and through adulthood, we allow our dreams to narrow or be extinguished? Why does our desire to take risks lessen? Why does the box we decide to live in get smaller, more enclosed, harder to see out of?

Thoughts of long-distance paddling have infiltrated my dreams for most of my life. Those dreams included the Mississippi and Yukon Rivers. And it was while I was thru-paddling the Tennessee River with my cousin Jeff in 2021 that I started dreaming about paddling the Ohio River. And shortly after I turned sixty-three years old, I began my Ohio River adventure.

Now granted, there are a great number of people who simply would never want to paddle the entire 981 miles of the Ohio River, or the 652-mile Tennessee River, or all 2,340 miles of the Mississippi. But there are also plenty of people who simply believe they can't, that the life they've created or that has been imposed on them won't allow it. That those kinds of dreams and adventures are for other people, not for them. That they don't have the time, stamina, money, or experience to do something that "out of the box."

I know because I've met these people along every river I've paddled, every long-distance trail I've hiked, and every multi-week bicycle trip I've pedaled. I've met dozens and dozens of people who have said, "I wish I could do what you're doing someday." I met some of them while paddling the Ohio River in 2024.

My grandson Rio believes he can be a gorilla someday. He just turned four years old a couple of months ago. At what age will the world tell him he's just dreaming the silly dreams of a little kid? At what age will he build a box that he'll climb inside and stop dreaming dreams and "thinking outside the box"?

GETTING AWAY FROM IT ALL

I'm always thinking about going on an adventure. My wife, Leslie, once told me that I am always either on an adventure or planning one. She was right; living in the moment is hard for me.

Before I actually embark on a particular adventure, I spend a lot of time dreaming about it. I imagine myself paddling down a specific river with my loaded canoe, or struggling through a mountain snowstorm towing a sled full of gear attached to my climbing harness. I feel the cold wind on my face, the fatigue in my muscles. I visualize myself in dozens of situations to know what the adventure will be like and how I will feel doing it. I picture the weather I'll face so I can plan what clothing to bring. I pore over maps to determine the distance between resupply points.

Some adventures I dream about for a year or two before I find a way to make them happen. But most of the time, I imagine and visualize an adventure for a decade or more. That's how long it can take for things in my life to line up enough to make that first paddle stroke on a big river or take the first step of a long hike.

The amount of time I spend daydreaming and planning on any given day depends on my mood, the time of day, and how long it's been since my last adventure. Since I last experienced physical pain and aching muscles. Since I last struggled to get through hours upon hours of mind-numbing boredom. Since I last felt true fear, knowing that if I lost my focus on the immediate moment, I could die. The more time that passes between adventures, the more my mind wanders.

If it's really been a while, then I know it's time to step out of my day-to-day life and get away from it all. I can feel when it's time.

When I sense I'm once again starting to take my life, my relationships, and my middle-class privilege for granted; when I've stopped appreciating the little things that bring me happiness and joy; when I'm spending more time being negative than content, I know it's time to go.

Dave Johnston was a team member of the first winter ascent of Denali in 1967. He wrote:

> It is by getting away from life
> that we can see it more clearly ...
> It's by depriving ourselves of the
> myriad of everyday experiences
> that we renew our appreciation for them:
> People's smiles
> Water running
> Children
> Warm rooms

Trees
Unfrozen boots and socks
My dogs
Indoor toilets
I've learned from my experiences.
I've learned that I love life.

KEEPING A SMALL FOCUS WHILE PADDLING A BIG RIVER

Sometimes life's challenges or our ambitions just seem too damned big. Too impossible. Too unattainable. Too stressful and overwhelming.

When a project, a task, or the circumstances seem too big, sometimes it helps me to just be in the moment and do the next thing. Instead of letting the next ten things overwhelm me, I just focus on the next thing.

"Next thing" thinking has also carried me through some excruciatingly long paddling days and some terrifying situations.

Now that my Ohio River adventure is over, I'm daydreaming about paddling the Missouri River. One of my "next things." I've been reading whatever I can get my hands on about others who have paddled the Missouri. In 2005, David Miller published *The Complete Paddler: A Guidebook for Paddling the Missouri River from the Headwaters to St. Louis, Missouri*. For the past twenty years, Miller's book has been the bible for anyone who is planning to attempt this epic, 2,341-mile paddling adventure. *The Complete Paddler* goes into extensive detail about virtually every mile of the river, including the towns and historic sites along the way. Miller also offers advice and gives a slew of suggestions about portaging around dams and paddling the massive reservoirs along the route.

Norm Miller (a different Miller) is generally considered the go-to source for information on thru-paddling the Missouri River.[1] In Miller's

---

1 Norm Miller maintains a fantastic website full of Missouri River paddler information at www.missouririverpaddlers.com.

2012 blog post for the website loveyourbigmuddy.com, titled "So, You Want to Paddle Down the Missouri River?," he describes the psychological and emotional challenges of long-distance solo paddling, particularly the difficulty of slowing down to "River Time" in a fast-paced world:

> In 2004 while paddling up the Missouri I was at a constant battle with myself. The main issue was the slow pace in which I moved. I could have easily walked much faster than I was paddling. In the strong currents of the lower river, [two miles per hour] was my [top] speed. So, living in the 20th century with all the high-speed, fast-paced lives we all live, slowing down to a snail's pace was very difficult. I had to concentrate on the small picture, never the final destination. My mantra was "one stroke at a time will get you to the ocean." I had to stay focused on the bend ahead, the distant tree or bridge and never the [final destination]! I would have gone insane had I not slowed my mind set. "River Time" is what many paddlers talk about.

Mark Spitzer, author of *Waterlogue: The First Canoeing Descent of North America's Longest River*,[2] another great book about thru-paddling the Missouri River, offers more sage advice by quoting Thoreau:

> I have learned this at least by my experiment: that if one advances confidently in the direction of his dreams and endeavors to live the life which he has imagined, he will meet with success unexpected in common hours.

Spitzer then goes on to quote Joseph Campbell:

2 *Waterlogue: The First Canoeing Descent of North America's Longest River* (2023) by Mark B. Spitzer is the other indispensable book I recommend all Missouri River thru-paddlers read. In 1989, Spitzer paddled from the utmost source of the Missouri River all the way to the Gulf of Mexico. He published his journals of this epic trip thirty-four years later.

> I say, follow your bliss and don't be afraid, and doors will open where you didn't know they were going to be.

And Spitzer concludes his book with:

> This is true. I confirm it. It can work at any age. Do your planning and do your homework, and of course it will work. If you have a dream or plan or aspiration, particularly if you are young, I can add this piece of advice: do it when you are 90% ready. Don't wait until you're 100% ready. That will never happen, and your life will wane away. Do it, and you'll find that helping hands are there.

PADDLING BIG RIVERS IN THE U.S.

Before you jump into reading about my Ohio River paddle in 2024, I have two closing thoughts:

First, I have several younger outdoor-adventurous friends in Alaska who are dubious about my tales of how amazing these thru-paddling trips have been on the Ohio, Mississippi, and Tennessee Rivers over the past several years. In their minds, these long rivers in the lower forty-eight are too urban, too tame, too populated, not remote enough.

It's true the 1,980-mile Yukon River, as well as the Noatak and Alagnak Rivers up north, are much more wild and remote and make for truly great thru-paddling adventures in their own right. But before you dismiss paddling the Ohio River as a cakewalk (which is like calling the standard route up Mt. Everest a "walk-up"), think about the last time you sat in your canoe or kayak for a full, eight-hour paddling day, and then think about getting up every morning and doing that day after day, for forty-seven days, in wind and rain, among big waves and big barges.

Then imagine the blue herons and amazing hillsides and forests you'll see along the way. The deer at the riverbank drinking water in the early-morning fog. That bald eagle that greets you for the first few miles almost every morning as you paddle through your sore shoulder muscles from the day before. Imagine sitting by a beach fire stoked with driftwood, sipping a glass of bourbon while you reflect on the day's adventures. Sure, it's different than paddling a remote arctic river. But it's still pretty cool.

Second, over the past six years, I've paddled the entire length of the Mississippi River (2019–2020), the Tennessee River (2021), and the Ohio River (2024). And every once in a while, someone asks me, "Why?" Why would I spend weeks and weeks sitting in a thirteen-foot canoe with sore muscles, away from home and from my wife, putting up with the wind and the waves, sleeping on the ground, sometimes feeling afraid, and often eating boring food? Why?

The best I can come up with is:

I like challenging myself.

I like seeing new things.

I like the person I am when I'm on an adventure.

And that's enough.

Ohio River
47 Days in Fall 2024

DAY 1

September 17, 2024

Confluence of Allegheny and Monongahela Rivers to Tevebaugh Run, Baden, PA

20 miles

Towns and locks: Emsworth Lock and Dam (6½), Dashields Lock and Dam (13), Leetsdale (14½), Ambridge (16½), Baden (20)

"You guys riding the trains?"

As we prepared to spend our first night on the right shoreline, at river mile 20, I realized we were only a few minutes' walk from a pizza place. So once our boats were out of the water, tents set up, and gear stowed away, my friend and adventure partner, VO, and I walked over to Monte Cello's Pizza ("Serving Pizza Since 1980") in the tiny riverside town of Baden, Pennsylvania.

We brought along our empty water bottles, phone chargers, journals, and maps. We were looking forward to spending the evening eating pizza, having a beer or two, charging our phones, and journaling about our first day on the Ohio River.

Monte Cello's, as it turned out, was delivery or takeout only: No tables, just a small bench outside the front window. No beer. No place to charge our phones. The young lady behind the counter informed us the nearest park with a picnic table was three-quarters of a mile away. Too far.

Once VO and I got our pizza and salads, I asked if we could fill up our water bottles. A young guy who seemed like the manager led us back through the pizza kitchen to a big sink.

As we filled our bottles, he stared at us kind of funny. "You guys riding the trains?"

I knew why he was asking. We were camped only fifty yards from a multi-rail train track, and seeing how scuzzy we looked after just one day on the Ohio River, he assumed we were riding the rails.

We told him we were on the first day of a forty-day paddle to the Mississippi River, although that didn't amaze him as much as hearing that we'd had to make our way through two locks and two dams in our small, self-propelled boats.

When his amazement had faded, the young man's eyes narrowed, and he asked a familiar question: "Why are you guys doing this?"

After only the first 20 miles of paddling, I wasn't sure myself. I was already sore, tired, and kind of bored. *Mile 20*, I thought, *out of 981 total miles!*

Sometimes self-doubt creeps in early.

Back at our tents, I plopped down in my green collapsible camping chair about four feet from the edge of the Ohio River, my belly full of salad and a decent meat lover's pizza. A slight breeze was coming out of the east, upriver —the same breeze I had been thankful for all day. The sun was setting, and the air was finally cooling off after hitting eighty-one degrees today.

In my other life, I reflected—my non-adventuring life—I spend so much of my time thinking about tomorrow, the weekend, next week, next month. Work stuff. Future trips I am always planning in my head. Paying bills. Politics. Whatever.

In that life, I am rarely present in the moment. More often than not, my mind is thinking about the future. Not good.

For me, trips like this—river trips, biking trips, hiking trips, climbing trips—are about spending time in the moment. Or maybe the moment that is coming up just around the next bend.

And in this moment, as the sun sets along the banks of the Ohio River, I feel at peace.

My day had started at 6 a.m., like usual, at our house in the Fineview neighborhood on Observatory Hill, on the north side of Pittsburgh. VO and his wife, Val, had spent the night at our house and were up at 7. Leslie was up sometime in between.

I caught up on a few work emails and tasks, then packed my lunch to eat later today on the water. Leslie and Val drove us down to the riverside next to the Pittsburgh Steelers football stadium (formally known as Three Rivers Stadium), and we were unloading our cars by 8:30.

Loading my thirteen-and-a-half-foot canoe had always been pretty easy. My five dry bags and packs were ready to go, so it was just a matter of carrying everything down to the river's edge and loading my boat. Then I tossed in the extras: paddle, spare paddle, map, bilge pump, coffee mug, portage wheels, a day bag that would sit between my legs, sunglasses, sunscreen, water, and my lunch.

It took VO longer to pack his kayak because he was stuffing ten to fifteen dry bags into his front and rear hatches. But even though this had been our first real opportunity to pack our boats, it didn't take long, and by 9:30 a.m., we were waving goodbye to our supportive wives.

It had taken us about eight hours to paddle the first 20 miles of the Ohio River. This included three short stops to get out of our boats and stretch, as well as time to "lock through" Emsworth Lock and Dam at mile 6.2 and Dashields Lock and Dam at mile 13.3, the first two of what would end up being twenty locks on the Ohio River between here and the Mighty Mississippi River. At each of these, the lockmaster directed us to paddle into the smaller of the two massive chambers. The smaller chambers take less time to fill and empty. We locked through both in only about thirty minutes each.

As we paddled up to Emsworth Lock, a huge tug that had passed us earlier in the day, with twelve rafted-up barges in its tow, was heading into the large chamber. But rather than making us wait, the lockmaster waved us into the smaller second chamber. The water drops for the two locks were eighteen feet and ten feet, respectively—small and relatively quick.

It was great to have Leslie see me off this morning. Typically when I start a big adventure, she isn't there. Well, that's not totally true. Leslie was there when I started the Mississippi and Tennessee Rivers. She was there at the start of three of my long-distance hikes, because we hiked them together: the Southwest Coast Path in England, the Wales Coast Path, and our hike across Ireland two years ago. And she was with me on all my long-distance bicycle trips, except for my cross-Mongolia bike trip last year. But this morning, it was nice to have her see us off.

Now, on the bank of the Ohio River, it was almost bedtime, and I hadn't thought one lick about tomorrow's paddle. It was too much. Almost too overwhelming. I needed to savor today, savor this moment. I needed to revel in the fact that we had paddled 20 miles today when the most I'd planned for was 18–19, that I wasn't feeling too sore, that the weather was perfect, and that VO and I were safe and dry.

If I started to think, "Shit, we still have 961 miles to go," I'd get anxious. Overwhelmed. Doubts would creep in. But if I just appreciated where I was right now, camping on the shore of the Ohio River with today's paddling behind me, I felt content, confident, and fulfilled.

Why couldn't I maintain this state of mind in my normal daily life?

Tomorrow would come soon enough, and I was excited to see what it had in store—other than a chance of rain, anyway. In the morning, we would get up and do this again. Then again, and again, and again.

It was more than two hundred years ago and about fifteen miles up the Monongahela River, in the town of Elizabeth, that Meriwether Lewis put his newly constructed keelboat in the river and headed down to the start of the Ohio River, then on to Clarksville, Indiana, where he and William Clark began their epic Corps of Discovery expedition.

How cool it was, I thought, to be paddling the first 981 miles of the Ohio River alongside the spirit of Lewis and Clark.

I looked at my watch. 7:15 p.m. I dug out my headlamp so I could read. Then I journaled, brushed my teeth, and read for all of three minutes before falling fast asleep.

DAY 2

September 18, 2024

Tevebaugh Run, Baden, PA, to Smith's Landing Campground in Chester, WV

23½ miles
Total: 43½ miles

Towns and locks: Beaver (26), Montgomery Lock and Dam (32), Chester (43)

I sat on a mowed grass lawn on the banks of the Ohio River. I'd marked this trailer park campground on the map months ago: Smith's Landing Campground.

More than eight hours of paddling had made for a long day. We paddled across the invisible line that separated Pennsylvania and Ohio on the right side of the river, and Pennsylvania and West Virginia on the left. We ended our paddle in Chester, West Virginia, about four miles past the state line. That was a long time to paddle a canoe.

We took two short breaks, one at mile 6 at a boat launch in Monaca, Pennsylvania, where I'd finished one of my day paddles a while back. Then we pulled off around mile 17 to stretch and rest a bit. In between, at mile 11½ for the day, we paddled into the Montgomery Lock and Dam, our third of the trip.

I was already pooped by the time we reached the lock, and it wasn't even our halfway point for the day. Once again, we paddled right into the smaller of the two chambers, and they locked us right through.

This morning, before we took off, I had cut my 100-foot bow line in half. I remembered being told paddlers needed a 100-foot line only for the first two locks, but not after that. So I cut my long rope in half and attached 50 feet to the bow of my canoe and 50 feet to the stern.

Well, it turned out I needed the whole 100 feet for lock number three.

As we paddled into the lock, a worker lowered a rope with a hook on the end and told us to loop our ropes over it. Then, he hauled up our rope ends, passed them around a large cleat up top, and lowered them back down to create a loop connecting us to the side of the lock chamber.

This procedure ensures our small boats don't drift into the middle of the chamber, or worse yet, toward the massive steel doors on each end. Once the rear doors close, the water in the chamber is drawn out, and our boats slowly drop to the water level on the downriver side.

But this time, as the water level got lower and I fed out more of my now-shortened bow line, I literally got to the end of my rope—and the water level was still dropping.

Fearing I'd have to let go, I scooted forward in my canoe and leaned over to untie the rope from the bow. I almost fell overboard, so I quickly sat back down. I had to let go of the rope I'd been holding as I tried desperately to cling to the slippery wall of the concrete chamber to keep from drifting into the center of the massive chamber. My rope was definitely too short. I shouldn't have cut it.

Just a little lock-and-dam drama.

Last night, we camped on a small, uneven spot along the river. My tent was only three feet from the river's edge, and our site was right next to several sets of very active railroad tracks, but it was the only flat-ish spot we could find along the river that late in the day.

Train after train passed all night long, blasting their loud train horns. And every time one started up from a dead stop, the couplers that connect each railcar clanked and groaned as they pushed and pulled against each other. I must've woken up twenty times during the night as those trains sped by just feet away.

I woke up around 5:45 a.m., still tired. It was pitch dark until 7, so I read my book, scrolled the news on my phone, checked emails, and wished for the sun to come up.

My favorite part of long-distance canoe trips is getting to the end of the day, taking off my wet shoes and socks, and putting on something dry. But my second favorite part is having coffee in the morning. As I sipped from my mug around 7:45 a.m., I hooted a few times because I didn't see or hear VO moving around in his tent and we'd agreed to be on the water by 8:30. We ended up launching at 8:50, which was not too bad for our first real morning on the river.

I was a little nervous about our plan to paddle 23½ miles on what was only Day 2 of our trip. That was a long way to paddle without a current to help us along. By mile 6, I was trying to stay focused and not feel dejected about still having so far to go.

Every day is a mind-over-matter challenge. While I paddle, I plan future adventures, turn on my tiny battery-powered radio, call my mom, and practice emptying my mind. I even made a couple of work calls today.

Once we reached mile 17 for the day, I could sense the end, and it was mentally easier to keep paddling. Like yesterday, we had a light breeze at our backs again, but it was still a long-ass day. Once we got the wind in our faces out of the west, it was clear that 23 miles wasn't going to be a realistic goal for the day.

I'd originally planned this trip thinking we'd paddle 25 miles a day for 40 days. But it was only Day 2 and I was already starting to think 20–22 miles a day might be more doable, which would mean a 45-day trip. I'd wait a while before breaking that news to Leslie, though. Who knew, I thought, maybe after a week or so on the river, 25 miles a day would be no problem.

The highlight of the day was Smith's Landing Campground, where we are now. I was a little concerned after we landed our boats and saw a couple dozen permanent trailers but no sites for transient campers like us, so we walked around looking for someone to ask for permission to set up our tents down by the water.

One large camper looked occupied, so I knocked. A super-friendly man answered the door. His name was Jim, and he was the "governor" of the campground. He said it was no problem for us to stay.

After we got set up on a grassy lawn near the river, a man who was probably in his mid-seventies drove down in a golf cart and introduced himself as George, the owner of the campground. He was wearing an American flag bandana. I was very aware that we were in West Virginia, a state that had voted for Donald Trump by thirty percentage points over Joe Biden in the last election. And there I was with a huge "Harris for President" bumper sticker on each side of my canoe.

George was very welcoming and friendly. He said lots of paddlers had camped here over the forty years he'd lived along the river. George asked if we drank Budweiser, then returned with four cold cans in an insulated bag.

Not long after, Jim showed up and asked if he could bring us some dinner. About forty-five minutes later, he came back with two steaming plates of roast pork loin with a bourbon-and-brown-sugar rub, portobello mushroom caps stuffed with sweet sausage, and brussels sprouts topped with melted parmesan cheese.

Unbelievably good.

Such a great end to a long day.

Jim and George stopped back down to see how we liked our meals, and we all chatted about the river, the barges, and the paddlers. I asked if they saw many thru-paddlers doing the entire Ohio River. George said he'd met a few over the years, but not every year.

They offered to build a bonfire near the water, but as nice as their offer was, it likely meant a late night—and more Budweiser—so we politely declined.

West Virginia ... who would've guessed?

DAY 3

September 19, 2024

Chester, WV, to Steubenville Marina

22½ miles
Total: 66 miles

Towns and locks: East Liverpool (44), Wellsville (48), New Cumberland Lock and Dam (54½), Toronto (59), Steubenville (66)

Today was long. Eight hours on the water was just a long time to be paddling.

Doubts filled my mind. I tried to get my head into some kind of Zen space—a no-thinking space—but it never lasted long. My mind wasn't strong enough. There really was no way to speed up the miles.

When I paddled hard and in rhythm, with no current and no wind, I could move my fully loaded, solo canoe about three and a half miles an hour. But once we started getting headwinds out of the west, the prevailing wind direction, things slowed down.

VO said today he thought I was a faster, stronger paddler than he was. I actually thought the opposite. I just paddled harder. VO took very fast and short strokes as he paddled his kayak. I had tried to keep up with his paddling cadence, but I couldn't do it. Since VO and I had never paddled together before, I knew it would take some time to get into some kind of traveling sync with each other.

Though both of us a kayak paddle to propel our boats, I take slower, longer strokes, reaching farther ahead and pulling farther back before bringing my paddle blade out of the water—one stroke for every one and a half of VO's.

I got up a little earlier today to get some computer work done. By

6:45 a.m., I was packing up the stuff inside my tent, and by 7, I was out the door.

The trailer park had a tiny camper nearby that served as a public bathroom. Jim and George had seemed very excited to tell us about it yesterday and offer it for our use. So we even had an indoor bathroom during our stay here!

I boiled some water and made a big mug of instant Starbucks with powdered milk, then settled into my camping chair to get some work done before VO was up and at 'em.

At 8:00, a shirtless older guy—who probably shouldn't have been walking around shirtless—wandered over from the marina next door. He said he had seen us pull up to the shore yesterday. His name was Dan, and he lived in a huge brick house up behind the marina. He asked a lot of questions about our trip and told us a bit about some of the river towns we'd be paddling past over the next few days.

Dan was a retired "boilermaker," and he made that known, just as George had the night before. In fact, Jim had also been quick to tell us he was a union steamfitter. It was interesting how all three of these guys introduced themselves by their union trades.

Dan told us about an Ohio River thru-paddler he'd met a few years ago who was paddling an aluminum canoe decked in plywood. What a sight that must have been! According to Dan, he carried all his supplies in five-gallon plastic buckets with covers while his dog sat up on the plywood. The guy claimed to have paddled the Mississippi River three times. He sounded like a crackpot to me.

Dan offered to boat us down the river a ways. We declined, of course, but he gave us his phone number in case we needed any help farther downriver. He had a pickup truck and said he'd drive us back to Pittsburgh if we decided to end our trip in the next several days. Nice offer, but today was only Day 3!

I launched about twenty minutes before VO this morning and floated around in the middle of the river, watching for barges and sipping my coffee.

We had beautiful scenery for much of the day today. Ohio was on the right, West Virginia on the left. The river cut deep into a valley, with forest on both sides for most of the way. We also passed several industrial plants.

Four or five tugs with barges passed us from behind. They were surprisingly quiet. Dan called them "silent killers."

It was supposed to hit eighty-two degrees today, which it did. My weather app predicted sunny with clear skies all day, so I loaded on the sunscreen. Thankfully, it was cloudy for at least half the day because the sun bouncing off the water created a roasting effect. VO was tucked into his kayak hatch and spray skirt, so he was not as exposed as I was. I dumped several cups of cold river water on my head and down my back to cool off. It was refreshing, but the cooling effect only lasted a minute.

No wind. No current. Just a lot of paddling.

I called my son Seth to see what he was up to, talked briefly with my ninety-two-year-old mom, then got ahold of Leslie toward the end of the day. The last couple of hours really dragged. I got spurts of energy, but today was a grind, plain and simple.

I did the math over and over in my head. Averaging 25 miles a day would take us 39 days. 20 miles a day, 49 days. 22–23 miles a day, 45 days. That was realistically what we'd be able to shoot for. So far it had been 20, 23, and 23, and tomorrow we were planning a 22-mile day. Wind, waves, and storms would all affect these academic calculations. Eight hours on the water left me, well, eight hours to think about this stuff.

I saw an immature bald eagle and lots of blue herons today. Fish were jumping all around me. It was really a peaceful day. Hot, but peaceful. It was nice to be away from the urban outskirts of Pittsburgh. I focused on gratitude.

Now, we were nearing Steubenville, Ohio. I'd written on the map that we'd stop at Steubenville Marina, but I had crossed out the word "marina" and written in "park."

Both terms were too generous. The marina was nothing more than a run-down, broken-up parking lot—the kind of place drug deals went down. A few cars were parked there, and a handful of people fished off the shore. It looked pretty depressing, actually. A tiny plot of parched dirt by the river seemed to be our only camping option, but there were no trees for shade, and it was still hot as hell.

Then I noticed two covered picnic pavilions up on a hill, above the parking lot. I got out of my boat and walked about five minutes uphill to find grass, several big shade trees, and some park benches and picnic tables. There were a few people milling around.

As far as parks went, this one was miserable. The single porta-potty was not only full to the brim, but shit was literally smeared all over the floor and walls. Nasty beyond description.

We strapped our portage wheels beneath our boats and towed them about six hundred yards up a fairly steep paved road. I had to stop several times to rest.

By 5:30 p.m., we were unloading our boats and pitching our tents on a grassy spot in the shade that overlooked the river, both of us totally exhausted from a very long day. We kept our boats right next to our tents and hoped we wouldn't get run off by the local police.

A quick check of Google Maps showed no restaurants within walking distance. And neither of us felt like cooking, so we used VO's DoorDash app and ordered a chicken meal for four with mashed potatoes, broccoli, and a half gallon of lemonade from a local Bob Evans.

It arrived in forty-five minutes. Brilliant! I'd never used DoorDash on a long-distance canoe trip before. We sat at a picnic table like civilized campers and had a nice dinner. Bob Evans had even sent along tomorrow's breakfast: a loaf of banana walnut bread.

By 8:30 p.m., it was pitch dark and getting chilly. My sleeping bag and the extra down blanket I had brought would keep me plenty warm.

Tomorrow would be eighty-three degrees and sunny. Another hot one, and another long day. But for now, safe and with full bellies, we relaxed to a beautiful view of the river. It was a good day.

I was proud of our effort.

DAY 4

September 20, 2024

Steubenville Marina to Martins Ferry, OH

22 miles
Total: 88 miles

Towns and locks: Wellsburg (74), Tiltonsville (82½), Pike Island Lock and Dam (84), Martins Ferry (88)

"Rumor has it one of you has a 'Harris for President' sticker on your boat."

I kiddingly denied it and pointed to VO.

Then I fessed up. "It's my canoe."

"You know where you are, don't you?"

Welcome to the Martins Ferry marina in Ohio.

Across the river was West Virginia. Trump Country. We'd only seen a few Trump and MAGA signs so far, and a few boats with Trump flags. But zero signs for Kamala Harris.

Getting up this morning was chilly, and a heavy fog sat on the water. It had dropped into the high fifties overnight. Stepping outside, I saw I had set up my tent beneath a tree that was dripping some kind of sticky fluid all night long, and my tent fly was covered with it.

For breakfast, we had the loaf of banana walnut bread from Bob Evans and instant Starbucks at our picnic table. Great start to the day.

We were on the water by 9. The river was like glass, and the scenery was beautiful. Perfectly calm. Zero current. Serene paddling.

It felt like we were zipping right along. Mile 8 came quickly. We pulled off at a boat ramp in Wellsburg, West Virginia. Had it been later in the day, it would've been a great lunch stop, with a restaurant right on the water.

I had slept well, and I felt stronger this morning. My body was starting to get used to this routine. But the heat was building and the sky was clear. I dumped countless cups of cold water over my head and down my back. It felt so good, even if just for a few seconds.

The next eight miles were a struggle, mostly because of the heat. There was one long stretch with no landmarks, just lots of unending forest. It was beautiful, but hard to stay motivated. I had a long call with my mom, which was fun. Talking to her always helps get me through the hard paddling stretches.

At mile 16, we stopped at Rayland Marina on the Ohio side. I'd been looking forward to it because my river guidebook noted a small store with beverages, and I really needed a break from the sun. But Rayland was a huge disappointment: No store. No cold drinks. Nothing.

I found a spigot and dunked my head under the cold, gushing water, then we sat under a covered picnic shelter, happy to get out of the sun.

After that, we paddled two and a half miles to Pike Island Lock and Dam. Once again, we called the lockmaster about fifteen minutes out and paddled right into the small chamber that he had prepared for us. I tied up on the shady side of the chamber, which gave me a nice break from the sun for twenty minutes or so.

The final four miles to the Martins Ferry marina were tough. Hot. Slow. The water felt thick, like paddling in honey. I pulled out my radio, tuned it to a local radio station, and powered through.

After a while I decided to video call Jeff, my paddling soulmate. Jeff and I had paddled the entire Mississippi and Tennessee Rivers together. That was a fun call. It brought back so many great paddling memories. Talking with Jeff helped me reconnect with how amazing it was to be on a long-distance adventure like this. And he got me through the final forty-five minutes. Jeff had really wanted to be on this trip, but he couldn't make it happen, so he was living through VO and me.

The marina turned out to be private. As we pulled up to the boat ramp, we passed a dozen beautiful yachts. On one of them, a guy was blasting music from Queen on his sound system, and I gave him a thumbs-up as I paddled past. Since he was the only person at the marina, I walked over to his boat after we pulled off just downriver and asked if we could set up tents for the night. We learned he was the "admiral" of the boat club. The man in charge.

His name was Craig, and he was super nice. Sure, we could set up our tents, he said. We could also use the showers, help ourselves to cold drinks in the fridge, use the covered outdoor kitchen, and eat dinner at the picnic tables. So nice!

Craig told us he'd boated up and down the Tennessee and Cumberland Rivers, as well as the entire Ohio River.

As soon as we got out of our boats, I made my way to the marina fridge and grabbed a couple of ice-cold beers that VO and I enjoyed while we unloaded our boats and set up our tents.

We had arrived at 5 p.m., and around 6:30, Craig gave us a ride to a nearby gas station that, according to him, had the best food in Martins Ferry. We each bought a huge hot sub sandwich and way-too-big salads. Despite how hungry I was after a long paddling day, I could only eat half the sandwich and less than half my salad.

After an amazing hot shower—the first in four days of sweating and sunscreen—I hand-washed the clothes I'd been wearing since we started and hung everything on a clothesline strung between a trailered boat and a fence post. I was sure it would all still be wet in the morning, but maybe it would dry strapped to the front of my boat tomorrow.

This trip is such a great way to stay focused on the moment. On the hour. One day at a time. We've paddled 88 miles and still have 900 to go, so it's best to just stay in the moment. Tomorrow we'll hit our 100-mile mark. That is something to celebrate, but thinking too far beyond the next day feels overwhelming.

As VO and I sat under the covered eating area at the marina, several marina club members stopped by to say hi. Craig had sent out a notice letting everyone know he'd given us permission to spend the night.

One guy, who went by Piggy, walked up to us while we were journaling. “Rumor has it,” he drawled, “one of you has a ‘Harris for President’ sticker on your boat.” I immediately pointed to VO, even though it was my canoe Piggy was talking about.

Piggy proceeded to turn the channel on the mounted television screen to Fox News. I knew that was no coincidence, but it was sort of funny. We made small talk with Piggy—about non-political topics—but I really wanted to get some journaling done.

Piggy said that some years, the river current runs four miles an hour, but this summer it wasn’t moving at all. Just our luck. No wonder we felt like we’d been working so hard all day long.

Today was my grandson Rio’s third birthday, so I made him a little birthday video from his Cha Cha.

DAY 5

September 21, 2024

Martins Ferry, OH, to Jeff the Mayor's backyard in Powhatan Point, OH

21 miles
Total: 109 miles

Towns and locks: Wheeling (90½), Shadyside (98), Moundsville (102), Powhatan (109)

It's 5:30 p.m. in Powhatan, Ohio, and Mark and Christine, our across-the-street neighbors in Pittsburgh, will be here any minute. They had wanted to meet us on the river sometime, and today, Saturday, worked for them.

We had hoped to paddle to the Powhatan Point public marina and park, located on Captina Creek just off the Ohio River, camp there, and meet up with Mark and Christine for an evening picnic. So last night I called the Powhatan Police Department to let them know we'd be camping at the park. Two hours later, Jeff, the mayor of Powhatan Point, left me a message saying the city council had passed a resolution prohibiting camping at the park. At that moment, he lost my vote.

Since there were no motels or Airbnbs in Powhatan, we'd just have to figure out what to do when we got there. Finding a place to camp along a river isn't always easy. The riverside is mostly private land, and the public spaces in riverside towns typically aren't amenable to camping.

I called Mayor Jeff back and left a message telling him we were thru-paddlers and asked if he had any suggestions for places to camp. As a last resort, we could ditch our boats somewhere and have Mark and

Christine drive us to a motel in another town, and we could Uber back to our boats the next morning.

I didn't sleep well at all last night. I couldn't fall asleep, which I blamed on the Diet Pepsi I had had for dinner with my monstrous sub sandwich. Then, starting at 5 a.m., I kept waking up every fifteen minutes. I finally gave in and read the news on my phone, checked emails, and stretched out my tent time until 6:45.

I had made VO promise we'd get on the water this morning by 8:30 to give us some extra time with my visiting neighbors. VO was awesome. Got up, got moving. We had portions of yesterday's sub sandwiches for breakfast with coffee, and we were on the water by 8:30.

Beautiful, cool morning. I love paddling at that time of day. There was a slight headwind of about five miles an hour.

We hit our 100-mile mark today. I originally had plans to celebrate somehow, but it was only mile 12 of our day, so we just paddled on through.

We paddled past Wheeling, West Virginia, on the left, and Wheeling Island on the right. The island had several huge Victorian mansions overlooking the water.

There was a lot of tug and barge traffic once we passed Wheeling, and we had to pay close attention to what the tugs were doing. They sure didn't slow down or make any attempt to avoid our tiny boats. It was on us to stay out of *their* way.

Around mile 6, I called for a short break as the breeze out of the southwest picked up to about ten miles an hour. We passed long stretches of forest on both sides of the river followed by several long-ago abandoned industrial sites. Maybe coal or cement. Lots of rusty metal pylons in the water for tugs to tie off on back in the day.

Miles 6–12 were tough for me. A headwind. Slow progress. Since there weren't many visual landmarks to see or look forward to, I switched on my little radio to listen to music, then changed to the Ohio State football game. They were leading 21–7 at the half against Marshall.

We stopped just past the town of Moundsville, West Virginia, around mile 14 for the day. I was exhausted from paddling into a wind that, by now, was blowing a steady ten miles an hour. I chowed down on the last section of yesterday's now-soggy sub sandwich and lay on a small patch of sand to stretch out my sixty-three-year-old lower back a bit.

Thunder rumbled in the distance as we were getting back into our boats, and I noticed big, black clouds to the north. I checked my weather app. A small thunderstorm had popped up just to the north of us. The sky got dark and the wind picked up, but confident the storm would stay to the north, we paddled off. We got soaked by two short bursts of heavy rain, but it felt great since the temps were in the low eighties. The laundry I had strapped to the outside of my spray deck to dry ... didn't.

After a couple of miles and two big bends in the river, we had a slight breeze at our backs for a few minutes. But then it whipped around 180 degrees and started blowing right into our faces at a steady twenty miles an hour, kicking up one-and-a-half-foot waves and white-caps that pounded us for the next two hours.

I was actually sort of into it.

The waves gave me something to focus on. Cutting through at a forty-five–degree angle, several waves crashed over my bow. I kept an eye on the shoreline so I wouldn't end up in the middle of the river and concentrated on not tipping over.

I dug my paddle blade in with every stroke and focused on increasing my pace and speed. I hated paddling hard into the wind and getting nowhere, so I paddled even harder for the next two hours. VO dropped off behind me. I steered toward the middle of the river a couple of times to look back and make sure he was still there.

This morning when I woke up, I had another voicemail from Mayor Jeff. He said we could camp in his front yard along the river tonight. It was a relief to have a place to stay and meet up with Mark and Christine. As we neared Powhatan, we started to see houses and yards, and eventually the "red brick house just after the A-frame with a metal dock" that the mayor had described. We had no problem finding it. We unloaded our boats and only carried up what we needed for the night.

We set up our tents in a sprawling, grassy lawn beneath some gigantic trees right along the river. Jeff came out to meet us as I was draping my wet laundry over the branches of a tree.

The second-term mayor of Powhatan was a fairly young guy, and super nice. He made us feel right at home. I had packed up a bunch of wet stuff this morning, so it was nice to dry out our tents, sleeping pads, and clothes.

We had decided on a picnic rather than going into town for dinner, so Mark and Christine showed up with prosciutto, various cheeses, baguettes, beer, salad, and grapes. It was a fantastic spread. We spent three wonderful hours sitting in our lawn chairs along the Ohio River, visiting, drinking beer, and eating great food. It was so nice to see them, and so great that they'd driven all this way to cheer us on.

By 8:45 p.m., the temperature was dropping. Once Mark and Christine had gone, I sat down in my camping chair and turned on my headlamp to write. It was weird to think they were heading back to their house in Pittsburgh, right across the street from my house, while we'd be crawling into our tents for a good night's sleep before starting Day 6 on the Ohio River.

DAY 6

September 22, 2024

Powhatan Point, OH, to Paden City, WV

24 miles
Total: 133 miles

Towns and locks: Clarington (118), Hannibal Lock and Dam (126), Paden City (133)

> *Leslie just dropped us off at the Paden City Campground. It's part of a beautiful city park on the water. We're the only people here, and I'm not even sure it's open.*

I looked up from my journal. It was only 7:40 p.m., and I already needed my headlamp to see the pages I was writing on. The days were getting shorter.

We had anticipated trouble today at the Hannibal Lock and Dam, about seventeen miles into our day. Apparently, the larger lock chamber at Hannibal was under repair and would be out of operation until December. All barge traffic had to pass through the small chamber, which meant that large barge tows had to be broken up into shorter sections and shuttled through. This could take several hours per barge. And when we paddled up, there were half a dozen barges ahead of us.

VO had called the lockmaster this morning, and the guy said he might be able to squeeze us in with one of the tugs they use to pull the broken-apart barges out the other side of the lock. But when we arrived at 2 p.m., the same guy said it would be six to eight hours before he could possibly get to us, but we could hang around in the water.

In anticipation of this river traffic jam, Leslie had agreed to drive almost two hours from home to help us out. We paddled right up to the Ohio side of the lock, with Leslie waiting on the shore, and it was easy to unload our boats and haul everything in two carloads to the other side.

The only place we could get back onto the river was at Fishing Creek, a little stream that drained into the Ohio. It was on the opposite shore, across a bridge on the West Virginia side. It took about an hour and a half to shuttle our gear and boats over to the creek and start paddling again. We paddled another five miles to Paden City Campground, where Leslie met us again and we all went out to dinner.

Our morning today had started in dense fog. When I crawled out of my tent a little after 7, VO was already outside boiling water for tea. We ate the rest of the yummy chicken salad and baguettes that Christine had brought the night before, and we were on the water by 8:45. Everything was wet from the heavy dew, and there was a thick fog hanging just above the water. I relished the chill in the air, knowing the predicted high of eighty-eight degrees was only a few hours away.

VO was a powerhouse this morning. I stopped paddling early to put on some sunscreen, find a radio station, nibble on some grapes and nuts, and text Leslie a few updates. But those brief lulls in paddling put me a good half mile behind VO, and it took me almost eight miles to catch up.

I actually wanted to stop and stretch around mile 8, then 9, then 10, then 12, but VO, who was still a ways ahead of me, showed no signs of slowing down. Finally, around mile 12 or 13, I caught up to him, and we found a swampy spot where we could get out of our boats for a stretch break.

Paddling conditions were great this morning. Flat calm. But it got hot just a couple of hours into the morning, and by 10 a.m., I was once again dumping cups of cold water over my head and down my back. The sun was relentless all day. It took its toll on me.

I saw some small fawns drinking by the river. Plenty of blue herons. And another curious bald eagle.

Around noon, I found the Steelers pregame show on my radio and ended up listening to the game into the second quarter before we met up with Leslie at the lock.

After we set up our tents at the city park and stowed our gear away, we drove five miles back to New Martinsville, near Fishing Creek, and had dinner at Choo Choo, a cafe that Leslie had scoped out. I had the Choo Choo burger and fries.

As Leslie left to head back home, she said she'd come back to the river in a week or so to spend the night in a hotel. Something to look forward to. Leslie's visit was too short, but I loved seeing her, and she really helped us out today. We were both glad she had made the trip.

There was rain in the forecast for the next three days—different intensities and durations depending on which weather app we checked. VO's app simply predicted "storms" tomorrow, but they all said rain over the next few days.

We'd shoot for the town of St. Marys, West Virginia, tomorrow. There was a crappy motel about five blocks off the river if we ended up being soaked all day. Otherwise, we could stay at a little city campground along the water at St. Marys. It's supposed to cool off a little tomorrow, with a high in the low eighties. I'll take it.

Seth took off for Alaska today with Arlo and Rio. It was the first time he'd traveled alone with both boys on an airplane. Back to Seth's childhood home in Sitka.

Time for bed.

DAY 7

September 23, 2024

Paden City, WV, to St. Marys, WV

22 miles
Total: 155 miles

Towns and locks: Sistersville (138), St. Marys (155)

We had quite a storm last night. It rained from 11 p.m. to 5 a.m. The rain came in three waves, but the middle one was the worst. High winds. Driving rain.

I was afraid a large branch from the tree I was camped beneath would come crashing down on my head. VO said this morning he was afraid his tent was going to collapse in the high winds.

Everything in my Big Agnes Copper Spur tent and vestibule stayed pretty dry. When it was really raining hard, there were several drops driving through the seams of my "waterproof" rain tarp and into my tent. The top of the tent was just mosquito netting, so once water penetrated the rain fly, it dripped onto me.

Rain had puddled on the seats of our picnic table, so I sat on my raincoat and fired up my small MSR Reactor camp stove to make coffee. Leslie had left us some biscotti that tasted amazing with my instant Starbucks.

VO discovered an outhouse on the other side of the park, a find we were both pretty excited about. Much better than pooping behind a tree.

Thankfully, the rain ended at 5 a.m. and it didn't rain for the rest of the day. It got a little misty a couple of times, but it was mostly cloudy and muggy, and the temperature hit eighty degrees in the afternoon.

The scenery was beautiful today. No big industrial sites, just forest and hills. And with the gray skies, the views from the water were amazing. The paddling was long, as usual. Around mile 5, I stopped to rest my arms a bit; at mile 9, we got out of our boats to stretch our legs; and at mile 14, we took a lunch break. But otherwise, we just kept paddling.

Like the last few days, we had a headwind. Initially, it was 2–3 miles an hour—not bad, but enough to make you work harder to keep up any kind of pace. Then it picked up to 10 miles an hour, which got exhausting after a good four hours. To stop paddling meant I would start drifting backward.

A bald eagle followed us for a while, and we saw two little river otters who popped their heads up and stretched their necks as far out of the water as they could to get a better look at us.

We pulled up to the concrete boat ramp at St. Marys city park, not sure if we were going to camp under a covered picnic shelter or find a way to haul our boats and gear eight blocks to the St. Marys Motel. Yesterday when I searched lodging options in St. Marys, the St. Claire Motel was the only option. And the first review I read said something like, "This is the grossest place I've ever stayed. Smells. Roaches. Stay away!!"

Getting out of my canoe on the boat ramp, I saw three old duffers sitting on lawn chairs in the parking lot next to their pickup trucks. One guy was actually sitting on a brown metal folding chair, like one you'd find in a church basement.

I wandered over and introduced myself, asking about our overnight options. These three guys looked like this was what they did all day, every day of the week: sit in their chairs next to their trucks and shoot the shit. They seemed to think we could set up our tents somewhere in the park. I said that given the weather forecast of more rain, and our soaking-wet tents, we weren't too excited about spending another night in the rain. And then packing up wet tomorrow and paddling through more rain.

I mentioned the St. Marys Motel. They said they couldn't vouch for it, but "it's the only motel we have in this town." At one point, the shaggiest, most obvious Trump-supporter-looking guy of the three, Barry, said, "Hey, I'll go get my pickup and give you and your boats a ride to the motel."

"Really?" I said. "That would be awesome. The problem will be getting everything back down to the river tomorrow morning."

"I'll run you back in the morning, then. Just tell me what time to come get you."

Amazing.

Barry jumped on his Harley and roared out of the parking lot to get his truck.

A few minutes later we were loading both of our boats, paddles, and gear into the back of Barry's pickup, which was already full of tools and miscellaneous junk. VO jumped in the back to make sure the boats didn't slide off, and I jumped in the cab.

As we drove the short eight blocks to the motel, I noticed Barry was wearing a bracelet made up of little square, white beads, with a letter on each bead. It spelled out, "H-A-R-R-I-S W-A-L-Z."

I couldn't believe it. Riding in an old pickup with a surefire redneck in West Virginia, and the redneck was wearing a Harris-Walz bracelet. I said, "Barry, where did you get that bracelet?"

"My daughter made it for me."

"Are you a Kamala Harris supporter?"

He grinned. "I love her."

Barry went on to say he hated Donald Trump mostly because he was a draft dodger and "hates his own generals."

Barry said he was probably the only Democrat in all of St. Marys, and his buddies made fun of him for it. Once we got to the motel, I showed Barry the "Harris for President" bumper stickers on my boat.

We unloaded our stuff in the run-down and stale—but clean—motel room. Barry said he'd be back at 8 in the morning to pick us up. What a pleasant and unexpected encounter.

The other unexpected event of the day was that VO's phone crapped out. After spending an hour on my phone trying to find a place where

VO could get a new phone, and finding out there were no taxis or Ubers in St. Marys, and that no taxis would come from another town to pick us up, VO offered a hundred dollars to the young Indian guy sitting behind the motel front desk to drive him to the nearest Verizon store in Parkersburg, twenty-one miles away. It was the only option.

I stayed back and dried out my tent, sleeping bag, and some clothes that I had washed in the shower. Wet stuff hung all over the room and outside on our chained-up canoes.

We've been paddling for seven days. One full week. And we've traveled 155 miles.

DAY 8

September 24, 2024

St. Marys, WV, to Boaz, WV

21 miles
Total: 176 miles

Towns and locks: Newport (156), Willow Island Lock and Dam (162), Marietta (172)

It was a soggy day, but way better than it could have been.

The forecast was for wind and rain all day, with the possibility of hail—and even a tornado—in the afternoon.

What we got was overcast and calm until 11 a.m., followed by two hours of heavy rain, but no real wind. The last two hours of our paddling day started with very light rain followed by a headwind that eventually picked up to about ten miles an hour. So, a little of everything, with the last couple of hours making for some hard work.

During the downpour, I paddled until I was soaked to the skin before I decided to put my raincoat on. Not sure what I was trying to prove. I think I just didn't believe it was going to keep raining for so long. The temperature got close to eighty degrees, so I never got chilled. Looking back on the day, I'm not even sure what the point of putting on my raincoat to begin with was.

Barry gave us a great sendoff this morning. He showed up at the motel promptly at 7:45. VO and I were all packed up and had just finished our McDonald's Egg McMuffins when he pulled up. Barry seemed so happy to see us and immediately gave us each a "Harris-Walz" beaded bracelet, just like the one he was wearing.

"My daughter was so excited to make these for you," Barry said, handing us our bracelets.

It was really touching that Barry and his daughter had thought to do this for us.

When Barry first pulled up this morning, I handed him a twenty-dollar bill, and he refused it, twice. He was just being kind. Helping two strangers out. He said, "I know that someone will help me out sometime in the future."

We loaded our boats and gear into the back of Barry's pickup while he sat and sipped his McDonald's coffee.

Back at the St. Marys city park boat ramp, Barry watched us pack up our boats. "I can't believe you can fit all that shit in your boats," he said.

Just before we pushed off, Barry gave us his phone number. "If you need any help down the river, or get into any trouble, call me," he said. "I probably won't drive all the way to the Mississippi River. That's too far. But anywhere between here and there, just call me." And I knew he meant it.

As we paddled away, I said to VO, "This is the reason I do these trips. Because I get to meet people like Barry. I actually don't really like the paddling all that much. But it's the Barrys that I'll remember for the rest of my life."

At mile 6, we got to Willow Island Lock and Dam, our seventh lock on the Ohio River. I called about a mile out and the lockmaster said he would get the chamber ready for us. It was always a nice break from paddling to bob around in a lock chamber for twenty minutes or so. As we left the lock and paddled downstream, we passed two tugs and tows heading upstream, waiting to lock through. Those were the only two boats we saw all day.

It was seventeen miles of paddling today to get to Marietta, Ohio, a real riverfront town with a huge levee to protect the town from flooding. We planned to stay at the historic Lafayette Hotel, built right along the river. VO and I were soaked from the rain by the time we arrived in

Marietta. We'd only stopped to get out of our boats once, just after the lock. Stopping for breaks in the driving rain didn't make sense, so we just kept paddling.

I typically like paddling in the rain. It gives my mind something to focus on, motivation to paddle harder. I talked with my mom for quite a while during the heaviest downpour, until I started to worry that my phone was getting too wet.

We pulled off the river onto the West Virginia bank just before Marietta to decide whether to continue on or stay put. If the predicted tornadoes and high winds were close, our plan was to pull our boats up at a public ramp right in front of the Lafayette Hotel. But the weather seemed to be holding off, so we had a late lunch snack and climbed back into our boats for another four miles past Marietta. The wind started to pick up a bit just as we pushed off again, but we knew that in an hour or so we'd be done for the day.

We stopped at what Google Maps identified as River Valley Campground in Boaz, West Virginia. We pulled off into a little slough at a broken-down boat dock with rotting deck boards where there were a couple of small, half-submerged boats tied off. VO got out and walked up a long flight of cracked wooden steps that led up the steep riverbank to the eight or so permanent trailers that made up the "campground." I could hear him from down below as he went from trailer to trailer knocking and yelling, "Hello?"

We were just hoping to pull our boats onto the abandoned dock and leave them for the night so we could head back to the comfort of the Lafayette Hotel. But we didn't want to leave our stuff without asking someone.

After about fifteen minutes, a lady drove up to her camper. Her name was Melissa, and she said this was a private campground but told us it would be fine if we pulled our boats up onto the rickety dock and tied them off for the night. We left most of our gear underneath our overturned boats, but I grabbed my clothes pack, day pack, electronics bag, map case, and a pair of dry shoes for the night.

From down below, I heard Melissa say to VO, "I'd be happy to give you guys a ride. How are you getting back to Marietta?"

"Uber," came VO's reply.

I yelled up the hill: "I like Melissa's idea better! We'd love to have a ride to town."

Melissa told us the trailers at River Valley Campground all belonged to extended family. She lived in a nice camper along the river that was surrounded—engulfed, really—by hundreds of lawn ornaments and rusted pieces of this and that, strewn all over. She and her husband lived in the camper nine or ten months out of the year. Melissa said that for the other two or three months, when it snowed, they moved back to their house about a mile up the road.

There was no shortage of "God Bless America" signs and American flags around the place. And hundreds of random wood and metal signs, pots and pans, plastic chairs, golf clubs, metal toys, empty flowerpots ... all kinds of things lying around. It was quite a collection. Melissa was exceptionally nice and friendly. She seemed more than willing to help two soggy old men who just showed up on her doorstep.

The Lafayette Hotel was a huge, historic hotel that was built in the mid-1800s. Black-and-white photos of old paddlewheelers hung on the walls of the lobby and dining room. Every room, including our bedroom, was full of aged, stately furniture. VO took a seat at an ornate, hand-carved writing desk in our bedroom to work on his journal.

We did our first load of laundry of the trip. The clothes I'd been rinsing out in the river and wearing every day were really starting to smell.

We had dinner at the hotel restaurant. Amazing salmon, asparagus, and mashed potatoes. We each had a couple of IPAs, and now I can hardly keep my eyes open as I write in my journal.

It was weird to think that just a couple of hours ago, we were soaked to the bone, paddling the Ohio River through wind, rain, and hail, and now I was sitting in my bed, warm and dry, in a historic hotel after a great meal—and that tomorrow morning we would just climb back into our boats and continue on down the river.

I dried out my tent last night in St. Marys, but VO has his draped around the hotel room tonight.

Scattered thunderstorms are predicted for tomorrow, so I'm sure we'll get wet and stay wet all day. We're camping tomorrow night for sure, so it could be a long, soggy day, ending with a long, soggy night. We are also supposed to have some headwinds in the afternoon.

We both agreed over our salmon dinner and beers that we'd take hotels like this any time we could get them. Why not?

DAY 9

September 25, 2024

Boaz, WV, to the boat ramp at mile 192 on the West Virginia shore

16 miles
Total: 192 miles

Towns and locks: Belpre (184), Parkersburg (184)

We changed our plans about ten times today. After a fantastic dinner, laundered clothes, a very comfortable bed, and a good night's sleep, I admitted I wasn't super psyched about getting going this morning. Our plan was to grab the free hotel breakfast at 7 a.m., get a hotel shuttle ride to our boats in Boaz around 8, and hopefully be on the water by 9.

That was before the thunderstorms rolled in late in the night. Before bed, we had seen predictions of lightning and rain through morning, but we both hoped the bad weather would turn south. I had checked my weather apps a few times during the night when I got up to pee to get rid of the thirty-two ounces of beer I'd drunk for dinner.

At 6 a.m., I fired up my laptop to get some work done, and at 7, I informed VO that the weather forecast hadn't changed. Thunder boomed outside the hotel as we discussed what to do.

With this stormy weather predicted for several more hours, we decided to enjoy our breakfast, relax, and catch a ride to our boats around 11 a.m. Even if we had to pack our boats in the rain, we could hopefully be on the water by noon. I picked a possible stopping point at a nameless boat ramp at river mile 192. That would be 16 miles for the day. It would set us even further behind our original goal of finishing the Ohio River in forty days, but being honest with myself, that goal had gone out the window a few days ago. After eight days of paddling, we were averaging exactly 22 miles a day. And this was paddling seven and a half to eight hours every day.

Today's 16 miles would set us back even further. But the weather was in charge today. If it were only raining, we'd be heading out right after breakfast.

I got a couple of solid hours of computer work done, which was great, but it only confirmed how far I'd fallen behind in my emails and other work-related things I needed to follow through on. This was mostly a working vacation, so I had a fair amount of pressure to stay on top of my work.

Around 9:30 a.m., our weather check showed the lightning was turning south of us, so we made a quick decision to leave the comfort of our nice hotel. This was unfortunate, because I'd been planning on a 10 a.m. nap.

The hotel shuttle guy didn't know the family campground where we'd stashed our boats. As we headed that way, VO and I disagreed on which road to turn off on, but as it turned out, we were both wrong.

Everything was where we'd left it. Melissa had already left for work, so we cut through her yard ornament menagerie and down the cracked and slippery wooden stairs to the even more decrepit dock. VO slipped and fell on his ass as he ventured down the stairs. Several of the dock boards were rotted through. The ol' family campground had fallen into a state of disrepair.

We had our boats packed and on the water by 10:45 a.m., a couple of hours later than usual. The River Valley Campground was on a little side channel of the Ohio River that was separated from the main river by Muskingum Island, a part of the Ohio River Islands National Wildlife Refuge. Dozens of islands that we'd paddled past over the last eight days are designated as part of the refuge, and as such, there is no camping allowed. There are even signs that say you need permission to step foot on the island, although we'd thought a few times about camping on one of the refuge islands and taking our chances of getting caught.

We had a headwind that blew straight out of the south, the direction we were heading in for most of the day. The headwind grew to a consistent ten to twelve miles an hour, with gusts in our faces for the next ten miles, making it a struggle to keep paddling into the wind and oncoming waves. It was nonstop. To keep paddling hour after hour, making minimal progress, was demoralizing, and it tested my ability to put my brain into neutral and just paddle. With every paddle stroke, I missed our cozy beds at the Lafayette more and more.

It was slow and exhausting work. And then it got dangerous: we needed to power across the river—from Parkersburg, West Viriginia, on the left side, to Belpre, Ohio, on the right.

Paddling across a big river in my little canoe with waves and whitecaps always makes me nervous and gets my adrenaline pumping. So I paddled as fast as I could to get across the middle and closer to shore. With the potential of a tug and tow around every corner, tipping over on a day like today would not only be a drag, but terrifying in waves like these. A tug captain would never see me.

When the river took a ninety-degree turn to the right (west), the wind was somehow still in our faces. I don't get how that works. It's like sitting by a campfire with the smoke following you around no matter where you move.

We eventually got some shelter by staying close to the four-mile-long Blennerhassett Island, which was actually a state park. We paddled past a small dock where a paddlewheel boat brought tourists over from Parkersburg. The state park has a horse-drawn covered wagon that takes people around the island. I wasn't sure what else there was at the park, but we could see cleared areas, hiking paths, and picnic tables.

We stopped for our second short break around 2:30 p.m. at one of the cleared areas of the park and had lunch snacks, which are always the same as our morning snacks. Then we paddled the final four miles to our planned stopping point, an unnamed boat ramp at river mile 192.

Above the concrete ramp was a nicely mown grassy area, a perfect spot to set up our tents. There were three huge, red-brick buildings on the edge of the grassy area that were completely overgrown with vines, with trees growing out of the caved-in roof. An older guy was parked nearby, and when he saw us pull up, he came over and offered us energy drinks.

His name was Richard, and he lived across the river in Ohio but said he came here every day to pick up litter and "straighten things up." He told us that the largest building, with its cupola and huge, glassless window openings, was an old lockhouse that generated power from a small hydroelectric dam that used to cross the river. The two other brick buildings were where the lock workers lived. Admiring these cool old pieces of history made me wonder why someone wasn't renovating them.

When we arrived at 4:30 p.m., it had been drizzling on and off for the past two and a half hours. It stopped long enough for me to make up a few tortillas with packaged hamburger, black beans, and cheese for dinner. We busted out a couple of warm Modelo beers that we'd been carrying since hanging out with Mark and Christine.

Sunset was at 7:15 p.m., so it would be dark soon. When it started drizzling again, I finished journaling in my tent.

VO and I were both worn out from the wind today, but VO seemed a bit down. He was usually so positive, but he seemed a little off tonight. Totally understandable.

We are hoping to paddle twenty-four miles to another boat ramp tomorrow, but it will all depend on the wind. My WillyWeather app seemed to be saying—if I was interpreting it correctly—that sometime tomorrow, the wind would start to come out of the east and northeast, which would mean at our backs. That would be fantastic.

DAY 10

September 26, 2024

Mile 192 to Sherman, WV

25 miles
Total: 217 miles

Towns and locks: Hockingport (199), Belleville Lock and Dam (204), Devil's Hole rock feature (210), Sherman (217)

Let's start with our unexpected encounter with the police, transition to waking up to early-morning fishermen and rain, follow with a paddling day that included our hurricane avoidance strategy, and end with what the hell we are planning to do next.

VO and I were in our tents by 7:00 last night. After I had finished my journaling, I read a little and fell asleep.

As I dozed off, I was aware of a few cars randomly driving to the boat ramp and turning around. None stayed for long. But around 9 p.m., a set of very bright headlights seemed to be pointing directly into my tent, not moving.

Then, a car door opening, footsteps, and a man's booming voice: "Who do we have here?"

I sat up, dazed. "Uh ... Jon?" I muttered.

"What are you doing here?"

"Camping. We're paddling the Ohio River."

"Can I see who I'm talking to? This is a police officer."

I unzipped the wet tent fly and stuck my head out of the tent door. The bright beam of a flashlight was trained right on my face.

"There's no camping allowed here, sir. Even fishermen have to be gone by sunset. There are signs posted all over."

"Really? I actually looked for 'no camping' signs when we pulled up. I even commented to my buddy how nice it was that camping was allowed."

"Well, there are at least three signs. One on this big, brown sign right next to your tent." The officer aimed his flashlight at the big, brown sign right next to my tent that said nothing about camping. "And another one down on that wooden post," he said, pointing his beam at a wooden post about seventy-five feet away that didn't even have a sign on it.

"I don't think this big, brown sign says anything about no camping," I said. "We both read it."

The cop walked over to the big, brown sign and pointed his flashlight at it, then walked toward the wooden post with no sign on it. "Well, there used to be signs here. I'll have to tell the office to bring more down. People are always tearing them down. There's a lot of drug use and partying going on down here every night."

He aimed his flashlight back into my face. "It's crazy," he said. "Every single night it's crazy down here."

I craned my neck through the tent door to look around. It was raining and crappy outside, with not a soul in sight but the three of us.

"Every night," the officer said again. "It's wild down here."

I sat back inside the tent. "Look, officer, we'll be out of here by 8 a.m. Heading down the river. You can see our boats over there. We're obviously not here to party."

His flashlight beam swept over the one remaining Modelo on my small camping table. "No alcohol allowed either."

"Outta sight, outta mind as far as the alcohol goes, sir." I gave a weak chuckle.

He ran his flashlight over the rest of the campsite. "Okay. Well, I guess I'll let you stay here just tonight, as long as you aren't wanted for anything." He pointed his flashlight at VO, who now had his tent open, too. "I'll need to see both of your IDs so I can run a check on you."

Are you fucking kidding me? I thought. *Boats, paddles, life jackets, two guys in their sixties camping in the rain?*

VO and I stretched our arms out of our tent doors with our driver's licenses.

In the ten long minutes it took for the cop to run our licenses, I started to worry about the time I got arrested in Washington, DC, for trespassing at Brett Kavanaugh's nomination hearings for the Supreme Court. VO said later he was worried about a parking ticket he never paid when he was in college.

Officer Numbnuts eventually wandered back to our tents and returned our licenses. He told us to be careful. He made sure we understood he was really going out on a limb to let us stay in our tents, in the pitch dark and rain, at 10 p.m., with nowhere else to go.

Asshole.

It rained for most of the night. Just a light drizzle, so when we crawled out of our tents around 7:15 a.m., everything was wet.

Two fishermen towing a bass boat drove up and asked what we were up to. They seemed amazed at our answer.

"I live around here," one of the guys said, "and I've never heard of anyone paddling this entire river." He pointed at my boat. "You're doing it in that canoe?"

"Yep."

He whistled softly. "Wow. You must have massive arms that I can't see from here."

"Nope."

As they backed their boat trailer down the ramp and into the water, they continued to talk about us. "God, I can't believe those guys," I could hear one of them saying. "I've heard of people doing the whole river in a houseboat, but never a canoe and a yak."

Their amazement pumped me up to get back on the river.

It had been raining on and off for the last few days, and it seemed like we were either paddling in the rain or camping in the rain. Or getting a hotel so we could dry out from being in the rain.

But today was a great paddling day. Overcast. Low seventies. Calm water at the beginning, then a small tailwind for the last four hours of the day. Muggy, but otherwise perfect weather for paddling.

Originally, the forecast showed light rain until 8 a.m. Then it changed to 10 a.m. Then again to show rain until noon. Ultimately, we paddled in a very light, misty rain for the first three hours or so.

Our goal was to paddle twenty-four miles to a boat ramp at an enclave of houses labeled "Portland" on the map, on the Ohio side. But as we paddled and I continued to monitor the weather, the reports I was hearing on my little radio were that the outer bands of Hurricane Helene, which was predicted to hit Florida as a Category 4 tonight, would bring rain and wind to our area all day tomorrow. They were talking about thirty- to forty-mile-an-hour winds.

All of this was confirmed by the fishermen we had met this morning, and the lockmaster at Belleville Lock and Dam at mile 12 today.

At one point, I heard on my radio that three West Virginia counties had already declared a state of emergency in anticipation of three to five inches of rain and flooding tomorrow. It was a vulnerable feeling being out on a big river knowing storms were heading our way.

By midafternoon, we were convinced we'd need to take tomorrow off. It was a tough decision for me because my mind was set on a forty-day trip, which had already turned out to be unrealistic given the river had no current this year. And 22–23 miles a day had so far meant being on the water for almost eight hours every single day. We'd heard that other years, and typically in the spring, the Ohio River flowed one to three miles an hour consistently. Just not this year.

Averaging 22 miles a day, it would take 45 days to get to the Mississippi, and now it looked like we'd have a zero-mile day tomorrow due to Hurricane Helene. I knew there was nothing we could do about it, but it was still disappointing to add days to an already long trip. 46 days would get us to the Mississippi on November 1.

We spent the day making a plan. We'd paddle to a spot on the map labeled Sherman, West Virginia. From the satellite imagery, it looked like Sherman consisted of a trailer park and a small, white church.

We paddled a little past Sherman and up into Little Sandy Creek to find a place to leave our boats where they would be out of sight—and out of the coming storm. We ended up at the only spot where the creek bank was flat enough to get out and unload, but it was super muddy. We grabbed what we'd need for a hotel stay and stowed everything else underneath our overturned boats. We were out of sight just below a rural road, across the street from that small, white church.

The next nearest town was Ravenswood, which was 5 miles away, but it didn't have any lodging, so we needed to get to Ripley, West Virginia, with its four hotels. That was 16 miles away, but we were confident Ripley would have either Uber or a taxi that could come pick us up.

We hauled our overnight bags up the slippery bank and walked out to the main road, West Virginia Route 68. Both VO and I tried our Uber and Lyft apps, but it turned out there were no rideshares anywhere around. The apps were so frustrating. They'd act like they were locating a driver with messages like, "Your driver's information will be sent to you in less than 15 minutes," or "Your driver will be located in 3–23 minutes." Then the time would expire with no further messages.

A few taxi services showed up in a Google search, but the nearest one was twenty-eight miles north in Parkersburg, and they weren't willing to come get us.

So at 5:30 p.m., we stuck our thumbs out on Route 68 and tried hitchhiking, now our only option. I told VO that if we didn't have a ride by 6:30, we should walk back and roll out our sleeping bags underneath the large overhang on the side of the little white church, then regroup in the morning. But knowing the outer rings of Hurricane Helene were coming our way, camping beneath an open pavilion seemed like one of the worst options.

Not a single car even slowed down for the next hour. I guess two old guys with arms full of dry bags hitching a ride in the middle of nowhere was not a very appealing sight.

Finally, VO walked back over to the side road where our canoes were stashed while I stayed out on the main road. Eventually a guy stopped and rolled his window down to ask VO if he needed help.

Introducing himself as Mark Gorman, he said we could get in. Mark didn't seem too enthusiastic, but we tried to make up for it with non-stop thank yous. He said he'd take us the five miles to Ravenswood, but we'd need to hitch the rest of the way to Ripley from there.

As we drove through Ravenswood, it started to rain. I asked Mark, "Could we pay you fifty dollars to drive us the rest of the way so we don't have to stand in the rain?"

Mark paused, then shrugged his shoulders. "I'll just take you the whole way," he said. It turned out his family was from Wilkinsburg, Pennsylvania, twenty minutes from Pittsburgh, where we had started this trip.

Mark was really nice. Super friendly. He drove us straight to a hotel and dropped us off. I handed him fifty dollars, but he refused it. Meanwhile, VO had slipped a fifty-dollar bill into his coffee cup holder without him noticing. Mark said he had to come back to Ripley tomorrow afternoon to get groceries if we wanted a ride back to our boats. We told him it would likely still be windy and rainy tomorrow afternoon, at least according to the forecast, so our plan was to spend tomorrow in Ripley and make our way back to our boats the following day.

"Here, take my phone number," Mark said. "I'm not going to promise I can take you back Saturday morning, but I might. Give me a call once you know your plans."

Leslie also offered to drive two hundred miles and spend Saturday night here—and maybe even Sunday night—to shuttle us around. So at least we had a plan. But as boxer Mike Tyson once said, "Everyone has a plan until they get punched in the mouth."

My last check of the weather at 9:30 p.m. showed rain and winds of twenty-five to thirty miles an hour until 5 p.m. tomorrow. So it looked like tomorrow would be our first zero-mile day. It would set us back a bit more, but it would be okay. We'd set our sights on a couple of twenty-five–mile days once the storm passed, since we'd be all rested up.

The good news? We passed the 200-mile mark today. And completed Day 10 of the trip.

DAY 11

September 27, 2024

Ripley, WV

Zero-mile day
Total: 217 miles

Well ...

We took today off.

In the morning, the weather seemed fine. Just drizzly. But by late morning, and into the afternoon, the wind increased and it rained harder. It probably would have been unsafe on the river, and crawling into wet tents tonight would have been uncomfortable and depressing.

I knew VO was feeling some strain about stretching this trip out even longer. We both were. We were still on a forty-five–day pace, but who knew what lay ahead.

One day at a time.

This morning, I spent some time planning out the next few days of paddling. I had a 25-mile day served up for us tomorrow, with a lock and dam toward the end of the day. After taking today off, I was hoping our bodies and minds would be up for 25 miles. The winds were predicted to be mild, like three to five miles an hour out of the south, which wouldn't hinder us too much.

I spent the entire day on my laptop and phone, catching up on numerous projects, emails, and phone messages. It felt good. For the past twenty-five years, I'd worked full time while squeezing in long-distance adventures, like paddling the Mississippi and Tennessee Rivers; climbing high points throughout Central and South America; hiking through Wales, England, and Ireland; and cycling across Mongolia,

Canada, and the eastern U.S. So I was used to juggling work and play. I'd been doing it my entire adult life.

I've always said to anyone who cared—and that isn't a very big group—that I wasn't going to wait until I was in my sixties to retire and travel. I was going to find ways to have adventures all along the way, starting with my first trip to climb Denali, thirty years ago. All that to say I've had to weave work into my adventures, at least when cell and internet service allows.

Some friends have said over the years that doing work on a trip like paddling the Ohio River for forty-five days would take away from the quality of the adventure. My response—or rationalization, perhaps—was that first, I wouldn't be able to do these long-distance adventures if I didn't do work along the way. And second, staying on top of my work actually eases my mind and helps me enjoy the trips more, because I'm not worried about coming home to a mountain of things I've been ignoring.

Regardless, it's just how I do it. My trip, my rules, as a paddler I met on the Mississippi River once put it.

While we had dinner at Cozumel, a Mexican restaurant right next to our Quality Inn, we got in touch with Mark, who agreed to come get us in the morning and take us back to our boats for fifty dollars. Fine with us. He'd pick us up at 8 a.m., and hopefully we'd be on the river by 9. It was supposed to rain on and off throughout the day tomorrow, with temperatures in the low seventies. Just fine for paddling.

Time to get moving. Get more miles under our belts. It's too early in the trip to think too far ahead, though that is exactly what I'm constantly fighting in my mind. It's hard for me to be in the moment.

Every day when I paddle, I focus on appreciating the moment. Focusing on the present moment and what I'm seeing and experiencing around me is what draws me to these adventures. They create time and space for me to be present.

One day at a time. One mile at a time. One paddle stroke at a time. One eagle, blue heron, deer, and tugboat at a time. We still have a lot of work and a lot of great experiences ahead of us.

DAY 12

September 28, 2024

Sherman, WV, to Old Lock 24 Campground

25 miles
Total: 242 miles

Towns and locks: Ravenswood (220½), Racine Lock and Dam (237½), Antiquity (240)

Looooong day!

But as usual, once the paddling was finished, the long hours seemed to quickly recede into distant memory.

I was up by 6:15 a.m. I grabbed my laptop and went to the hotel breakfast room to check emails and let VO sleep a little longer. I had tossed and turned a lot last night and got up to pee at least four times. The thirty-two–ounce beer and all the ice water I had at the Mexican restaurant were most likely part of the problem.

Our pseudo–Uber driver, Mark, showed up at 8:15 a.m. We'd been sitting out in front of the hotel for half an hour hoping he'd come early so we could get going. Mark was super apologetic while handing us each a ziplock bag full of freshly made granola. It was still warm. Mark said he had added dried apple, various dried berries, walnuts, and lots of other tasty ingredients. VO and I both dipped into our bags throughout today's paddle, and it was amazingly good!

Mark dropped us off in Sherman, where we'd ditched our boats two afternoons ago. Back down the steep, muddy embankment we went (VO slipped and fell on his ass again) to the muddy creekside that, because of the rain, was even muddier than when we were last here. Our boats and gear were still where we'd left them, but some animal had torn apart the two large ziplock bags of garbage I didn't want to hitchhike with and had left underneath my canoe. The few pieces of rotting prosciutto in one of the bags must have attracted a varmint.

We planned to paddle twenty-five miles today. That was a daunting goal on this river and was hard to fire up for. But we'd have almost perfect paddling conditions all day today. Slight to no breeze. Overcast. Mid-seventies.

This stretch of the river was very rural. Hardly any industry the entire way. It was Saturday, so there were several bass fishermen on the water and a few tugs pushing barges in both directions. But generally, it was a quiet river.

Our morning eagle leaped out of a tree as soon as we started paddling. This had literally happened every single morning of our trip. Almost always just one eagle, who would then follow us along the river. And always in the morning.

We only stopped twice today. Once around river mile 7, and again around mile 15. Both short, twenty-minute breaks to stretch, stand up, and give our butts a break. And eat some snacks. This time, it was fresh-made granola. During our second break, I lay down for a bit, just to close my eyes and stretch.

West Virginia was still on the left, and Ohio on the right. It didn't seem quite as hilly on this stretch of the Ohio River. Lots of sandy places to pull off. Very different from the first week of paddling, where for miles it was hard to find a single level spot to pull off.

I tried to find the West Virginia college football game on my radio, but I couldn't find it, so I resigned myself to listening to country music. I did find a good rock music station toward the end of the day.

I broke down my eight-hour paddling day into short goals. Sometimes it was paddling hard for 100–200 strokes. Other times it was listening to the radio for a while or calling my mom or Seth to chat. And sometimes it was just focusing on the trees, the blue herons that seemed to be everywhere, or the hundreds of geese.

We arrived at the Racine Lock and Dam at mile 20, and once again, locked right through. And then paddled on for five more miles. It seemed to take forever to reach our destination, the Old Lock 24 Campground, but at 5 p.m., after eight full hours of paddling, we finally arrived at the campground boat ramp. We were exhausted. And we still needed to unload, set up camp, cook, and eat.

I heaved my canoe onto the ramp and walked up to the old, three-story, red-brick lockhouse, climbed some concrete stairs, and walked through a wide-open door into a huge room that was full of mismatched furniture, piles of books, life jackets, and other assorted, strange items. It looked like a massive garage sale.

Eight old, overstuffed easy chairs were arranged in a semicircle in front of a large, wall-mounted television.

"Hello?" I called out.

No one seemed to be home, despite the front door being wide open. The lower level of the lockhouse looked like a repair shop, with parts of cars and trucks lying all over, along with rusty folding chairs, sections of boat frames, and who knew what else.

"Hello? Anybody here?"

To the left of the building was a huge garden full of all kinds of plants, but most noticeably, dozens of tomato plants with hundreds of overripe and rotting tomatoes falling off their vines and littering the ground. In the middle of it was a woman on her hands and knees. She stood up, hands covered in dirt, and waved at us.

Her name was Kirsten, and she and her husband, Eric, live in the decommissioned lockhouse and run the campground.

Kirsten wore a tie-dyed shirt. Her hair was all over the place. Her eyes sparkled with a hint of mischief. And I liked her instantly. She told me later her nickname was Chaos.

Kirsten told me a lot of things during our twenty-minute introduction, but she mostly talked about her "theme garden." This year, the theme was music. Last year, her theme was beets, and she had planted dozens of beet plants in honor of a friend of hers. So this year, Kirsten decided to build on the beets theme ("beats"—get it?) and planted a music garden.

Her garden patches were:

Heavy metal: Black, blue, and purple vegetables
Blues: Blue cabbage and lavender
Latin: Tomatillos and tomatoes
Rock 'n' roll: Vegetables that were round, like potatoes and acorn squash
Country: The only plant I remember was "horse" radish
Classical: "String" beans and other things I also can't remember

(We covered a lot of ground in twenty minutes, and I didn't sit down to journal until a few hours later.)

The whole theme-garden idea was absolutely brilliant. And hearing Kirsten describe the plants she chose to go with each music genre was fascinating. She was quirky for sure. And super warm and friendly.

I paid Kirsten twenty dollars and she let us camp at an open campsite, right next to a big motorhome with a permanent awning that covered a big concrete slab. It was supposed to rain all night, so she said we could stay under the awning to get out of the impending wet weather.

We hauled our bags up from the boat ramp and took over the entire covered space. The people who owned the motorhome apparently weren't coming back for a few weeks.

I opened the large, blue dry bag that had all my big camping stuff (tent, sleeping bag, sleeping pad) and pulled out one last can of Modelo that had somehow gotten punctured and soaked everything in my dry bag with beer. Apparently, my sleeping bag stuff sack, tent, inflatable pad, and camp chair had all been bathing in beer for the past two days. But we had the perfect place to lay everything out where it would hopefully dry.

I took a shower at the shower house. Then, I fried up a can of Spam and made a package of noodles alfredo and mixed it all together. It wasn't as good as I'd imagined when I packed that meal.

VO and I busted out our respective bottles of bourbon (we each carry one at all times) and had a couple of shots while we sat and journaled at the picnic table under the awning. Kirsten stopped by around 8 p.m. to check on us. VO offered her some bourbon, so she sat down to chat for a while.

Kirsten told us about living along the river, and the history of Lockhouse #24, and the new clean-coal–fired electricity plant across the river, and the solar panel manufacturing plant downriver, and her time living in Denmark, and what it was like when the Ohio River flooded out the campground, and much, much more.

She described herself as a "contrarian" who tended to do the opposite of what other people did, or expected her to do.

Chaos.

Time for bed.

Good day.

Long day.

Hard paddling day.

Satisfying day.

Content.

The Allegheny and Monongahela Rivers converge to form the Ohio River

Loaded up and ready to start a 981-mile adventure

My love and biggest supporter

Our first lock and dam at river mile 6½

Looking for a place to camp, Day 1

Smith's Landing Campground, Day 2

Around river mile 50 in case anyone wants to join

Camped at a park on the edge of Steubenville, Ohio, Day 3

Water like glass, Day 4

My canoe with its shameless Kamala Harris bumper sticker

Friends Mark and Christine join us for dinner at Powhatan Point, Day 5

The Ohio River isn't just cities and barges. This is around river mile 145

Getting a ride from Barry to the St. Marys Motel in St. Marys, West Virginia, Day 7

Barry, our river angel in disguise

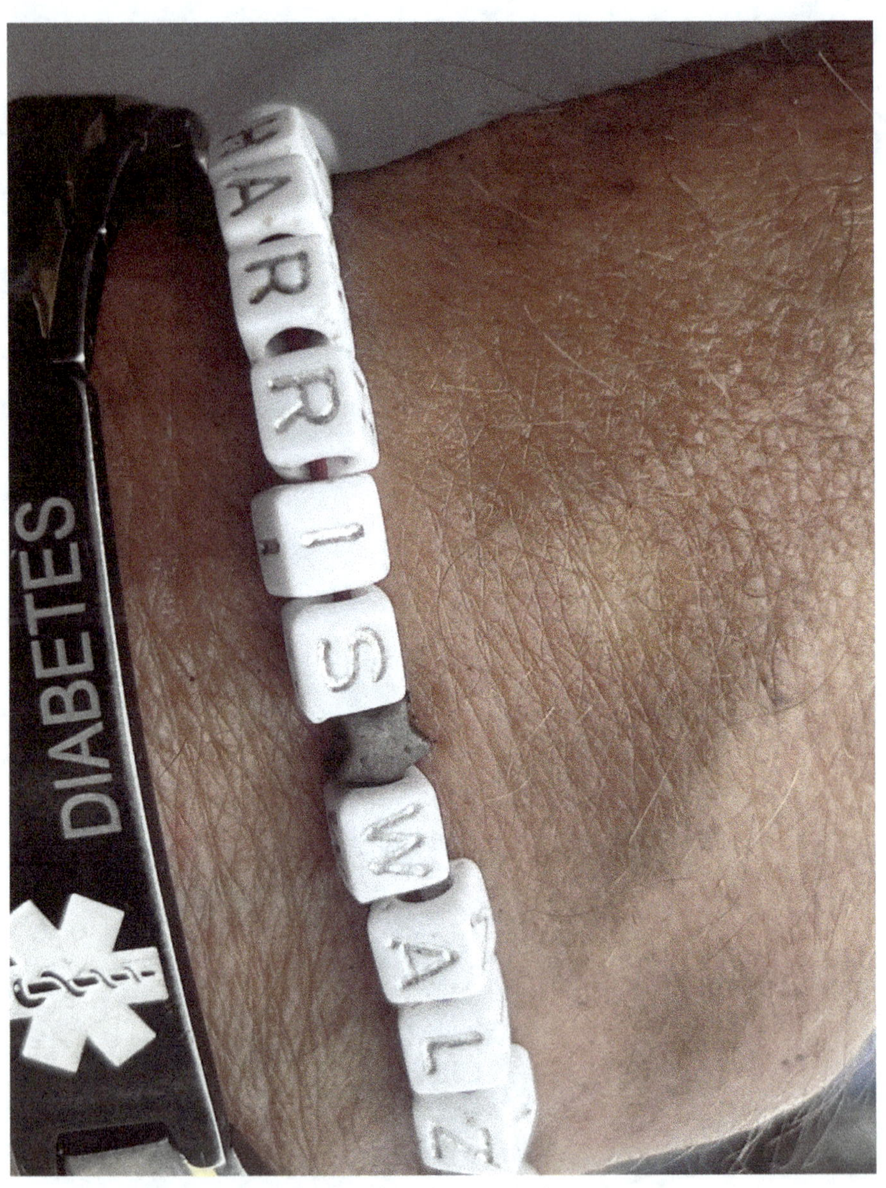

Barry tells us he thinks he's the only registered Democrat in St. Marys

Paddling in the rain on Day 8

The site where we got busted by the local sheriff for illegal camping, Day 9

VO scares up a flock of Canada geese

River traffic on the Ohio, Day 12

Barge graffiti near Ripley, West Virginia

The river town of Pomeroy, Ohio, Day 13

Campsite on Lesage Island, Day 14

VO demonstrating his fire-building skills

Any guesses as to what this means?

Hanging out in the Robert C. Byrd lock as the water level drops, Day 14

The first of over a hundred basketballs we saw floating in the river near Ashland, Kentucky, Day 16

Paddling alongside a tied-up barge

Leslie joins us to play our beer-tasting game in Huntington, West Virginia

Go ahead and think it: "That is a damned good-looking sandwich"

Sunset at our campsite in Portsmouth, Ohio, Day 17

We paddled in heavy morning fog on several days during the trip

Most tugs don't move in heavy fog. But there is always one ...

Peaceful night

Setting up camp at mile 383, Day 18

Just a cool damned sunset

My favorite whiskey of the trip

Just a couple of old guys on Day 19 of a canoe trip

DAY 13

September 29, 2024

Old Lock 24 Campground to Point Pleasant, WV

23 miles
Total: 265 miles

Towns and locks: Pomeroy (250), Middleport (252), Point Pleasant (265)

I just decided on the title for this Ohio River book: *I Want to Be a Gorilla When I'm a Grown-Up: 47 Days on the Ohio River*.

I know, it's a long title.

Rio, my two-year-old grandson, told his mom, Shauna, the other day, "I want to be a gorilla when I grow up." Ever since Shauna told me that, I'd thought about what a great metaphor that phrase is. I could be whatever I wanted to be. No limits. I could dream whatever I wanted to dream and set goals that other people might think were silly, or stupid, or impossible.

What would you do if you didn't have to follow predetermined norms or limits? Paddle the Ohio River, maybe?

It had rained all night long, so we were happy to be sleeping under a trailer awning. VO had set his tent up on the concrete pad right next to the big camper, and everything had stayed dry. I had just rolled my Therm-a-Rest air mattress—which now smelled like a brewery—and sleeping bag onto the concrete and had a very comfortable night's sleep.

After I got all packed up, I walked to the campground bathrooms to poop and saw Kirsten up at the big, brick lockhouse.

"How are you doing on your to-do list this morning?" I asked her.

“Well, I woke up,” she said, “but I haven’t had my shower yet. So I’m already half done for the day.”

I was starting to understand why she kept her to-do list short and manageable. Last night, she had said, “I used to get so down on myself when I couldn’t get everything done that was on my list. Now that my list is just ‘wake up and shower,’ I feel a sense of accomplishment every day.”

VO and I decided to just head down to our boats and pack up in the rain, rather than waiting for it to stop. We were soaked before we even launched.

Kirsten came over to see us off. She handed us each a small ziplock bag with two colorful campground brochures; two homemade cookies; and a slip of paper with her name, email address, and phone number. A note at the bottom said, “Adventure Groupie.”

“I think you guys are really cool,” Kirsten declared as we shoved off. “It was great to meet you.”

We actually had a slight current today, maybe one mile an hour for the first six hours or so. That helped push us along another half mile an hour, but it was great. After only two hours, we’d paddled almost eight miles.

It drizzled all morning. The shades of gray and green were beautiful. At mile 9, we passed Pomeroy, Ohio, a cute river town with an old main street, from what we could see from the water. I wish we’d taken some time to stop and explore. But even if we kept cruising along with our eight- to nine-hour paddling days, we were still on a forty-five–day trip. Long!

We paddled mostly through rural areas and past a few farms, two massive clean-coal plants, and a little bit of barge traffic. But all in all, a quiet river.

We were moving along so well that we decided we’d try to pass our 23-mile goal for today and go another few miles to Gallipolis, Ohio. But as we neared our 23-mile mark, I scanned Google Maps and our printed maps, and I just couldn’t find a place to pull off to either camp or find a motel anywhere near Gallipolis.

So we pulled off at mile 23, accomplishing our goal by 4 p.m. We stopped at a boat ramp next to an industrial yard and some heavy equipment. I knew there was a Quality Inn nearby, so I went to scout out a way to walk there while we stored our canoes down by the river. I walked through the industrial yard and up toward the road.

"Hey, what are you doing?" A man stomped aggressively toward me, obviously not wanting me on his property on a Sunday afternoon. He mellowed out after I told him about our trip, but several times he said things like, "The way things are these days, you can't trust anyone" and "The way this country is going, people will steal anything." Then he topped it off with, "Even older guys like you could be drug dealers or drug addicts."

Old, sopping wet, bedraggled guys who'd just climbed out of heavily loaded canoes? I wasn't sure about that.

At 7 p.m., we got pizza at the gas station next to our Quality Inn. We each had an IPA, then I did a small load of laundry, mostly to dry out clothes for tomorrow. After that, I was ready for bed.

Today had gone by quickly, and the miles had passed quickly, too. But twenty-three miles was still a long way to paddle. And being wet all day also made me tired.

Leslie is coming to meet us in two days! I can't wait.

DAY 14

September 30, 2024

Point Pleasant, WV, to Lesage Island

24 miles
Total: 289 miles

Towns and locks: Gallipolis (269), Robert C. Byrd Lock and Dam (279)

Great paddling day. We'd had a very slight current due to the rain the last few days, but it was enough to give us an extra half-mile-an-hour push. By 3:30 p.m., we had twenty-four miles in.

This was our first day with no rain in the last six days, and it was nice to end the day in dry clothes.

The paddling was beautiful. We passed the cute river town of Gallipolis, Ohio, at mile 4. A main street with lots of old buildings ran parallel to the river.

It stayed overcast all day, so even though the high temperature was seventy-six degrees, it never felt too hot. I did dunk my Green Bay Packers hat in the water twice, putting it back on my head and letting the cold water run down my back. I love that feeling when it's hot out.

We locked through the Robert C. Byrd Lock and Dam at mile 14. A big tug with ten barges locked through the larger of the two chambers at the same time we were using the smaller chamber. It was our tenth lock and dam of the trip, and once again, no problems. We had called about a mile out and the lockmaster said he'd have the chamber ready for us when we got there. And he did. Great service for two tiny, self-propelled boats.

We stopped three times for short breaks but still got to the boat ramp we had planned to stop at by 3 p.m. It was a trashy spot with no level place to set up our tents, so we decided to keep paddling.

I've noticed that for a day or two before we reach a lock, the riverbanks are steep with very few places to get out of our boats, let alone camp. This is because when the locks were built, the water level was raised on the upriver side of the dam, and artificial stone walls were constructed to keep the soil from washing away.

But for the first day or so of paddling on the downriver side of each dam, there were hundreds of places to stop and pull off the river, and many more level camping options. So, when we pulled away from our planned camping spot at the Guyan Creek boat ramp, I was confident we'd find a place to camp downstream, since we'd just passed a lock nine miles back.

We ended up stopping at the head of Lesage Island for the night. We got two extra miles in and camped on a nice gravelly beach. The tent options weren't super level, but the scenery was spectacular—definitely our best campsite yet.

With a nice campfire going, we sat in our collapsible chairs right on the riverbank and sipped bourbon. (I must have poured too much because I was feeling a little tipsy, and it wasn't even dinnertime yet.)

"We haven't taken the opportunity to do this yet," I said to VO. "Get to camp a little early and just relax by the river and enjoy the beauty." It was our first campfire of the trip.

This is Day 14. Leslie is planning to meet us tomorrow, so I am excited to get to Huntington, West Virginia.

Tomorrow, we'll hit 300 miles. But I am already looking ahead to Cincinnati, then to mile 490½—our halfway point—then to the Indiana border. These milestones help keep me motivated.

Just as I was thinking we hadn't seen an eagle all day, a beautiful, mottled, brown-and-white immature bald eagle took off from a tree just a hundred feet away.

Time to collect some more driftwood for the fire.

DAY 15

October 1, 2024

Lesage Island to Huntington, WV

20 miles
Total: 309 miles

Towns and locks: Guyandotte (305), Huntington (309)

We had a great campfire last night with all the driftwood I collected. There was plenty along the riverbank. The wood was wet from the rain this past week, but I found lots of dry twigs that were off the ground, and some dry bark. No pine trees or birch bark anywhere around. VO and I both tried in earnest to get the wet wood started but were initially unsuccessful.

VO eventually fired up his camp stove, which burned a bit like a blowtorch, and got a fire going. It was great to sit by a fire along the riverbank as the sun went down.

There were a few tiny mosquitoes out. The first of the trip. Sort of weird for this late in the year.

Today our goal was to paddle to Huntington, West Virginia, and meet up with Leslie. I'd already reserved two rooms at the DoubleTree hotel, which was just three blocks from the river.

I was wide awake at 6 a.m., so I read some news on my phone. My morning camping routine on the Ohio had been to start packing the stuff inside my tent around 6:45 a.m. just to get everything packed and organized: my sleeping bag and pad, clothes that were strewn about, book, journal, and headlamp.

When we had started our trip, the sun was coming up around 7, which gave me just enough light to slip outside and fire up my MSR Reactor stove for coffee.

But fourteen days into the trip it was still pitch dark at 7. I checked my weather app and learned that sunrise would be at 7:20 today. As we moved into October, the days were getting shorter.

VO had asked me last night if it was supposed to rain overnight. It was, but it didn't. My app was showing only a seven percent chance of rain this morning.

Fifteen minutes after waking up, and just after I'd finished packing up everything in my tent and was about to slip outside to face the day, it started raining. And hard! So much for seven percent. It poured for about twenty minutes, so we stayed in our tents until the worst of it was over.

On the river, I felt strong today. Once I had paddled through my achy shoulders and arms, which always takes a while in the morning, I was fine. I had taken off about fifteen minutes ahead of VO, fully confident he'd catch me in no time.

The wind picked up for the last hour or two of paddling. Even on those days that go by quickly and where I feel strong, 20 miles is still a long way to paddle. We got to Scott Waterfront Park by 2:30, our earliest stop of the trip. Since Leslie wasn't arriving from Pittsburgh until 4:00, VO and I decided to paddle another 4–5 miles. But I just couldn't see anywhere on the map after Huntington where we could meet Leslie to shuttle our boats to the hotel and back again in the morning. So we pulled off at the Huntington boat ramp at the riverfront park and ended our paddling earlier than planned.

There were a handful of curious folks who stood and watched us unload bag after bag from our boats. VO stayed behind while I took an Uber to the DoubleTree to drop off our bags, then paid the driver in cash to bring me back to the boat ramp. VO and I walked out into the water, positioned each of our boats on their small trailer wheels, and tightened the straps to haul them out of the water. We turned more than a few heads as we pulled our boats down sidewalks and across streets, diligently waiting at each crosswalk for the stoplight to change.

Once we'd checked in to the DoubleTree, I spread out my tent, rain fly, and some clothes to dry. Then I spent the rest of the afternoon and early evening hanging out with Leslie—and driving VO around to find a second replacement for his Verizon phone, which had crapped out again yesterday.

We ended up at a brewpub called The Peddler for great beers and sandwiches, then converged in our hotel room to watch the vice presidential debate between Tim Walz and J.D. Vance.

We all thought Walz did great—and that Vance was one smooth-talking liar.

DAY 16

October 2, 2024

Huntington, WV, to the marina in Worthington, KY

22 miles
Total: 331 miles

Towns and locks: South Point/Virginia Point Park (317), Ashland (323), Ironton (327)

Highlights of the day:

- Enjoying Starbucks in the morning.
- Crossing the West Virginia and Kentucky border on the left side of the river. No more West Virginia. Yeah!
- Going out for beers at Summit Beer Station and a great dinner at Black Sheep Burrito and Brews.
- Seeing over forty basketballs floating along the sides of the river. True story.

Early in the paddling day, around Ashland, Kentucky, I noticed a full-size basketball floating amongst the driftwood and other river garbage. A couple of minutes later, I saw another basketball, then another, and another.

VO and I started counting them out loud: *12 ... 13 ... 14 ...*

Most were regulation-size, orange basketballs. But some were blue; others red, white, and blue. Spalding balls. Wilson balls. Some were brand new, others old and worn out.

"It *is* Kentucky," VO said, noticing all the balls were along the Kentucky side of the river. "You know, of college basketball fame." He had a point. It was weird that we hadn't seen any balls until after we'd passed the Kentucky state line.

Then we drifted past a kickball. And a football. I was about to tell VO I'd found a floating softball when he spotted a soccer ball. Then a second one.

It was the craziest thing ever. In all, we paddled past over forty basketballs, three footballs, six soccer balls, and a softball, all in a stretch of only seven or eight miles.

What could have caused all these balls to end up on this one section of the Ohio River? I'd never seen any basketballs on previous river trips or even in other parts of this river—although about a week ago I did see some neon-yellow tennis balls floating on the side of the river. I counted ten within a few-mile stretch.

Miles 8–11, we paddled through a really congested section of the river, with dozens of barges tied together on both banks, and a bunch of tugs tied up together. We passed several coal and sand plants and encountered swiftly moving tugs pushing barges as they crisscrossed the river. We really had to pay attention to the barge traffic and crosscurrents. They certainly weren't paying attention to us.

The combination of a headwind, slight current, and all the barge and tug traffic caused waves that rolled back and forth across the river in every direction. These waves then smashed against the metal hulls of the hundreds of parked barges and made the water even more chaotic and hard to paddle through. My little canoe bounced all over the place, and my heart was in my throat the entire time. Tipping over in these treacherous conditions would be bad, especially with all the tugboats zipping around us.

Tense. Nervous. Focused.

The final three hours of paddling were into a fierce headwind of ten to fifteen miles an hour. It was relentless. The middle of the river was covered in whitecaps, and it did not let up.

We paddled hard through the waves, counting basketballs as we went. If it weren't for basketball spotting distracting me from the wind and waves, my mood and attitude would've really taken a nosedive.

Worthington's marina was a run-down shithole of a marina. None of the ten liveaboard boats even seemed habitable. Boat motors were covered in moss, and grass and small trees were growing on boat decks and roofs. Heaps of miscellaneous junk stood outside many of the boats, and from what I could see passing by on my canoe, the insides of several of them were piled high with clutter and garbage as well.

The wood of the docks was rotting, with some of the boards broken or missing. Because past storms had brought in silt that was never dredged out, the water around the docks was super shallow, in some places only a foot deep.

As we pulled up to the part of the rickety dock that was closest to land, a dog started barking. A disheveled guy came out of one of the houseboats to yell at the dog. Then he noticed us. We asked him if we could tie off our boats here for the night, and he said it would be okay.

Then a couple pulled up in a van that looked like the *Scooby Doo* Mystery Machine. When they saw us unloading our boats, they came over to tell us we weren't allowed on the dock because it was unsafe. They said they had to sign a waiver just to be able to live in their boat, which was tied off at the end of the dock.

It felt like a bunch of homeless people living in nasty, dilapidated boats. The guy that told us we couldn't walk on the dock called the slumlord marina owner to talk with us. He said we could leave our boats along the shore, but under no circumstances should we be walking on the dangerous dock.

I asked the van people what it was like to live here, and one lady told us it got really cold in the winter, and said it was especially scary when it flooded.

Yet people still lived here—year-round!

DAY 17

October 3, 2024

Worthington marina to Portsmouth, OH

26 miles
Total: 357 miles

Towns and locks: Greenup (336), Greenup Lock and Dam (341), Portsmouth (357)

Meow.

Meow.

Meow.

We started the day paddling through dense fog, staying a stone's throw from the riverbank. When the fog is this thick, we have to hug the shoreline because things like tugboats and giant barges can pop up out of nowhere and crush little boaters like us.

In the middle of this fog, I thought I heard a cat crying in the distance. Or was it some kind of strange bird call? Either way, we both heard it and paddled closer to the shore. That was when I saw this cute white cat on the shoreline, about fifty feet up the bank in some dense ground cover, meowing away. At first I thought she might be stuck or hurt. But as we paddled up to the shore, she came bounding through the foliage to the water's edge.

There she stood, just bellowing away. The saddest meows I'd ever heard.

She wasn't full grown and looked healthy. No scrapes or apparent injuries. She just stood on the shore and meowed away. She even dipped her paw in the water, considering whether to swim out to our boats. For a brief moment, I thought about rescuing her and having a cat mascot for the rest of the trip. Twenty-eight days paddling with a kitten in my canoe.

But since she looked healthy, and paddling for twenty-eight days with a kitten in my canoe was a really dumb idea, we decided to keep paddling, the sound of her crying as we paddled off echoing in my brain.

The weather this morning when we started out at 9 a.m. to when we pulled off the river at 4 p.m. couldn't have been more different. Leslie dropped us off this morning back at the Worthington marina in a fog as thick as pea soup. We could see fifty yards ahead at best. The air was cool and damp. Except for the fog, it was perfect paddling weather, with a temperature of fifty-four degrees.

Thankfully, we didn't have to paddle through any industrial areas with heavy boat traffic this morning. It would have been too dangerous. Tugs aren't supposed to travel in dense fog, but I'd seen it before on the Mississippi and Tennessee Rivers. We'd hear a tug engine somewhere out in the fog and have no idea how close it was.

At one point this morning, we paddled past a tug. There was a man up on the bridge, and I asked him if tugs were moving in this fog today. "They aren't supposed to," he said, "but there's always that one guy."

So because of that "one guy," we hugged the shore all morning. I thought it was cool paddling through the fog. We never saw the opposite shore of the river, the Ohio side. It was sort of mesmerizing. I could only see what was immediately around me. I took some great photos of VO paddling out of the fog toward me.

By 11 a.m., the fog was burning off. Around noon, at mile 10, we reached Greenup Lock and Dam. The name sounded like what a foreman would be yelling at a bunch of thick-headed workers who didn't know how to lay sod.

VO was frustrated with me this morning. I had packed my boat quickly, just like every other morning, and I told him I'd paddle slowly and definitely not cross to the other side of the river without him. Then I took off.

About thirty minutes later I got a text saying, "Where the hell are you?" I called back and said I was close to the shore, paddling slowly, and that there was no way he could miss me. VO hung up without saying anything, so I knew he was pissed.

I called Leslie, who was driving back to Pittsburgh, to confess my guilt for paddling too far ahead of VO. She told me I should never have paddled off and left VO behind in those foggy conditions. She said it was unsafe and made me promise to apologize to VO. So I stopped paddling and just hung out for about ten minutes before he paddled up.

The first thing VO said was, "I'm going to call you out on this one."

Oops.

When I had taken off, he thought I was just going to paddle out of the marina and not venture too far out into the river. Apparently, he had paddled around the marina looking for me and of course couldn't find me because of the fog, and because I wasn't there. And he was pretty pissed. Or at least very annoyed. And maybe a bit worried.

I apologized again, and we moved on. My bad.

After the Greenup Lock and Dam, we picked up a current, and for the rest of the day, we clipped along at a good four miles an hour. Between it only taking thirty minutes to get through the lock, and only taking one butt-stretch lunch break after that, we got just under twenty-six miles in by 4 p.m. In less than seven hours of paddling.

I'd picked three options for stopping points before we headed out this morning. A boat ramp at mile 23 just before the town of Portsmouth, a boat ramp at mile 24 at a city park right in town, and then what I noted on my map as a campground just after Portsmouth, around mile 25. Since we were making good time today, we eventually opted for the campground and the extra mileage.

The campground turned out to be a huge grassy area on the outskirts of an oval dirt racetrack at Portsmouth Raceway Park. When we got out of our boats to look around, there wasn't a camper or trailer to be seen. The aerial shot I had seen on Google Maps must've been taken when there was a race going on and lots of people had brought their campers.

We found a spot to set up our tents that was near the river but out of sight from any passersby. Of which there had been none this evening. It had been a cloudless day, with afternoon temperatures in the mid-seventies.

Glasses of bourbon in hand, we both sat journaling. Twenty-six miles for the day brought a wonderful feeling and sense of accomplishment. Leslie had seen us off this morning. I got to talk with Seth on the phone. Moved right through the lock with no delay. It couldn't have been a more perfect day on the Ohio River.

DAY 18

October 4, 2024

Portsmouth, OH, to river mile 383 (a mile past Quicks Run creek)

26 miles
Total: 383 miles

Towns and locks: Quincy (367), Vanceburg (378)

We were getting close to the 400-mile mark. That seemed like a milestone. I knew the halfway point, 490½ miles, would be even bigger psychologically. That was when the countdown would begin.

Right now, we were five days from the halfway point. That would be Day 23 of the trip. After taking a day off for Hurricane Helene, we were still on a 45-day pace. VO was hoping for more like 43 days. We'll see.

The sun didn't come up until almost 7:30 this morning. Today was October 4, and I could feel the days getting shorter. It was super foggy again this morning, so it felt darker than it was. Packing up and eating breakfast in the dark was no fun. To get going before the sun came up was a mountaineering thing, not a canoeing thing. But I realized the last couple of weeks of this trip, we would need to be ready to go before the sun was fully up, or at least be having breakfast in the dark, just to get on the water at a decent time.

The sun would set at 7:10 tonight, and it was already 6:50, so there wasn't much daylight left.

VO bought two more bottles of whiskey this afternoon. Last night, we finished off the Redemption Rye that I had started the trip with. And we'd finish off VO's Uncle Nearest 1884 tonight. Neither of us are big drinkers, as evidenced by the fact that it took eighteen days for each of us to drink a bottle of whiskey. VO busted open his bottle of 1792 Small Batch. Really tasty! He also bought a bottle of Elijah Craig, so we were set.

Sitting in our camp chairs, journaling at the end of a long paddling day, sometimes by a fire, with a tumbler of whiskey to sip on was one of the small pleasures of long-distance paddling.

Since the fog was so heavy this morning, our tents were soaking wet. Just dripping with dew. It was about fifty degrees when we crawled out this morning, so I was a bit chilly waiting for the sun to burn off the fog. Even though I was on the water by 8:45 a.m., I didn't dare head down the river alone after yesterday morning's trauma.

The sun coming up through the Portsmouth bridge and the dense fog was beautiful.

The fog wasn't as thick as yesterday, but it was still heavy enough that a tug with barges had pulled off to the side of the river to wait for it to burn off. The tugboat driver had pushed a corner of one of the front barges into the shoreline and kept his engines running to give a slight push toward the shore to keep the tow in place.

We paddled past just as the fog was lifting, and the captain waved to us from the fourth-story bridge. I still suggested we not cross the river until the fog had totally dissipated.

The current was not as strong today, but still helpful. No breeze. My weather app said, "Winds at 1 mph, gusting to 2 mph." Seriously? The word "gusting" shouldn't have been in the same sentence as "2 mph."

Lots of eagles this morning. At one point, an adult bald eagle and an immature one were chasing each other around. We saw at least eight eagles along the way today.

The temperature felt comfortable and cool until around noon, then it got hot. It hit eighty-one degrees, and the sky was cloudless. I'd decided to stop dipping my Packers cap in the water to cool off because every time I did, it would stay soaking wet all evening and into the next morning. No fun donning a wet hat on a chilly morning. So instead, I filled my coffee mug with cold river water and dumped it on my head and down my back a few times. It's taken me three long-distance canoe trips, totaling 140 days, to figure out that using my coffee cup is a better idea.

We took a lunch break around 1 p.m. I added honey to my lunch staple of a tortilla with peanut butter. Nice addition.

Mile 21½ brought us to Vanceburg, Kentucky, by 3:15 p.m., where I assumed—and kind of hoped—we'd be spending the night. Right on the water was Veteran's Memorial Park, with a nice grassy area and a big gazebo.

I'd used Google Maps to scope out Riverbend Pub & Grill, which was about a block from the river. We pulled our boats off the river at the park and walked up a hill into the cute little town of Vanceburg. As we walked into the pub, we got some stares from the locals at the bar who all knew each other.

The bartender, B.G., was friendly, and VO and I each ordered a cold beer. B.G. rattled off the dinner special: red beans, cornbread, sausage with sauerkraut, and diced grilled potatoes.

VO and I discussed our options. We could have another beer, eat dinner, and camp at the park tonight, which was my preference, or grab dinner to go and keep paddling, which was his preference.

There were four others sitting at the bar: an older couple who seemed weirded out that two total strangers had come into *their* Riverbend with the nerve to sit at *their* bar, an older guy, Gus, and a woman, Melinda, who turned out to be B.G.'s sister.

We asked them if they knew of any place to camp farther down the river, maybe 3–4 miles. Gus mentioned an island where he said they used to camp as kids, but on my map it looked like more than 8 miles downriver. Too far for this late in the day.

The tiny town of Rome, Ohio, complete with one post office and nothing else, had a boat ramp and was about five miles farther downriver. The other guy at the bar, the quiet one, thought it might be okay to camp there. On Google Maps, the spot he described looked like someone's front yard.

Then Gus lit up, remembering this great camping spot just two or three miles down the river. "Look for the big rocks," he said. "It's right next to them big rocks."

"Are there flat spots to set up a tent?" I asked.

"Yes. Definitely. We used to go there to party."

When? I thought. *In the 1940s?*

Against my better judgment, we decided to press on this afternoon with our takeout red-beans-and-rice dinners. I didn't really care, I was just feeling lazy and hated passing up a nice grassy camping spot next to a bar. But VO wanted to keep moving.

We asked B.G. if there was a place to buy whiskey nearby. There was a place, but even though it was less than half a mile away, it was too far to walk roundtrip and still get on the river to keep paddling. Besides, we didn't need to restock that bad.

As we were discussing this, Melinda chimed in from the end of the bar. "I'll drive you over there," she said. "Let's go."

"Don't worry," B.G. said without missing a beat. "She won't hurt you."

I stayed back and ordered two dinner specials to go—and hoped I'd see VO again someday.

We were back on the water at 4:45 p.m. We paddled and paddled and never did see Gus's great camp spot with the nice flat beach. Then again, I wasn't sure how long ol' Gus had been sitting at the bar before we'd gotten there. His mind may have been a little foggy. I'd scoped out a backup option that on the Google satellite photo looked like an unpaved road leading from a gravel or sand company to the river, so that was where we pulled off.

Mile 26 for the day. We found a level, gravelly spot a little ways up from the shore and set up our tents. It was already getting late with our stop in Vanceburg. I gathered up some firewood, and we sat down to eat our takeout dinner special by the fire.

The home fries were fine, but the cornbread was super salty, and the red beans had no flavor. And it was all buried under a mountain of sauerkraut—way too much, given there were only two or three small pieces of hot dog mixed in. It was a far cry from the "spicy sausage and sauerkraut" B.G. had described. The Riverbend "special" was truly awful.

And we devoured every single bite.

With my glass of 1792, it was the perfect end to the night.

A long day but a good day. We got miles in and had a nice break in Vanceburg, Kentucky, with B.G., Melinda, Gus, and the crabby couple.

Before I had left the Riverbend Pub & Grill to keep paddling, B.G. said, "It's definitely okay if you set up your tents at Veteran's Park down below the bar." He tipped his head toward the door. "The two ladies who just walked in are on the City Council, and they just voted that you could stay if you want."

DAY 19

October 5, 2024

Mile 383 to Maysville, KY

24 miles
Total: 407 miles

Towns and locks: Manchester (397), Maysville (407½)

"Experiencing humanity during inhumane times."

This was Leslie's suggestion for the title of my Ohio River book if I ever published one. She wrote that after I'd texted her about how much Trey and Jeff, two guys we met at the Maysville River Park Campground, had just helped us out.

We'd paddled twenty-four miles—a long day of paddling on a river with little to no current—to Maysville, Kentucky, where we found a small public park, public boat dock, and a city-owned campground a little ways off the water.

We unloaded our boats at the ramp, and I carried my empty canoe up to a grassy spot by some public restrooms. Then we looked around for a place we could lock our boats together for the night. Our plan was to call a taxi to take us and our gear to the French Quarter Inn, a historic hotel on the water in Maysville.

I saw a guy driving a golf cart around and waved hello. He stopped above the boat ramp and watched us unload, so I walked over and introduced myself. His name was Jeff, and he had the wickedest Kentuckian accent I'd ever heard. He'd spent the last twenty summers at the Maysville River Park Campground and seemed like the unofficial campground host. He even looked like an old family friend, Orville.

I told Jeff what we were up to and asked if there was a place to store our boats. He suggested we pull them up to the campground. They'd be safe there, he told me. In the same breath, Jeff said he'd be happy to drive us into town to the French Quarter Inn.

He zipped his cart back to his trailer and returned in a big, red Dodge truck. It was pulling a flatbed trailer, so we could load our gear onto that instead of lugging everything on our boat trailers all the way around to the backside of the campground. When he pulled up, Jeff was on the phone with Trey, the campground manager, to make sure it was okay to store our stuff. Minutes later, Trey arrived in his golf cart.

Trey told me to hop on the back of the cart and hang on to my canoe bow line, and he drove me the final several hundred yards with my boat in tow. Then he went back and did the same for VO and his kayak.

With our boats safe and secure, and our bags loaded onto Jeff's trailer, Jeff and Trey drove us to the French Quarter Inn, which we found out was fully booked due to a wedding. The only other downtown hotel, the historic Lee House Inn, was also full. Alas, the cute downtown O'Rourke's Pub that I'd set my sights on for dinner and beers had gone out the window.

Jeff and Trey graciously drove us four miles to the DoubleTree hotel in uptown Maysville. It was a little disappointing, location-wise, but perfectly fine. We had laundry, a good-looking breakfast, and a Tumbleweed Grill next door.

After a few minutes, our hotel room looked like a bomb had gone off. We had tents hanging from the curtain rods, wet dry bags scattered around. My sleeping bag and down blanket were on my bed airing out. Piles of laundry waited to be folded. It was all good, just a colossal mess.

After settling into our room, we wandered over to the Tumbleweed. VO and I each had two Painkiller cocktails on empty stomachs before dinner, which made me a little woozy.

This morning, I stayed in my tent until 7:00. The sun didn't rise until 7:33, but it started to get light enough to pack up inside my tent by

7. Super thick fog again this morning, for the third day in a row. Just about all the items we had left outside overnight, including rain flies and tent bottoms, were dripping wet—except my camp chair. After cooking breakfast a few times in a soaking-wet chair, I had learned to keep it under the tent vestibule at night.

Breakfast was two packets of oatmeal with a fistful of Craisins and freeze-dried raspberries stirred in. And of course, a big mug of instant Starbucks. My morning routine.

I enjoyed paddling in the heavy fog. The water was flat calm, and the fog lingered on the water for a good two hours. At one point, a tug pushing several barges came toward us and passed by. We could just barely make it out in the fog. Seemed pretty dumb to be pushing loaded barges through such dense fog, but like the boat captain told us the other day, there's always that one guy.

A few eagles graced us again this morning.

No shoreline industry today. We never saw the little town of Rome as we paddled past. Too foggy. We passed Manchester, Ohio, but otherwise, our twenty-four miles today were rural. Wooded. Today was October 5, and the leaves were just barely starting to turn color.

We had a slight tailwind all day, but no noticeable current. The closer we got to the next lock, what little current we had always seemed to disappear. Hopefully we'd get one again after locking through tomorrow morning.

Good day. Twenty-four miles. Clean laundry. Drying tents.

P.S. We passed our four-hundred–mile mark in the early afternoon today. Halfway on the Ohio River is just around the corner!

DAY 20

October 6, 2024

Maysville, KY, to mile 429 at Turtle Creek

22 miles
Total: 429 miles

Towns and locks: Ripley (417½), Augusta (427)

We were taking a break around mile 14 for the day when VO, who was standing down by the shoreline, had a remarkable epiphany.

"I just realized that when you pee on a hill, it runs down into your shoes!" he yelled up to me.

Good to know, I thought. I had been lying in the grass with my eyes closed, wishing we were done paddling for the day.

Later, I shared an observation of my own. "I haven't seen a single turtle on this trip," I said. "Twenty days and not a single turtle. Isn't that weird?"

VO said he'd already seen three. *Damn it.*

That evening, we set up camp on a flat, postage stamp–size spot in a little estuary, where Turtle Creek entered the Ohio River. It was the only spot we could find after paddling around and looking for forty-five minutes. We were in tall grass down below a train track. A pretty crappy camping spot, but better than anything else we'd seen.

Way off in the distance, some guy was talking into a microphone. I could tell he was an M.C. at a wedding because I heard the words "bride" and "groom." Just when you thought you were in the wilderness.

VO and I sat in our camp chairs sipping Elijah Craig whiskey and bragging about our sons, Seth and Steven, who are both pilots for

American Airlines. And Tyler, who is a successful business owner. A mellow end to what was basically a bullshit day.

It's always nice to be at the end of the paddling day with dry socks and shoes, tent set up, sleeping bag rolled out, sun setting. Just a nice time of day—at least when it isn't raining.

We had only paddled 22 miles today. We were shooting for 25, but I had secretly been hoping we'd stop at the 20-mile point for the day, at Augusta, Kentucky, which looked like a cute river town.

This morning was perfect. A taxi picked us up at the DoubleTree at 8:00, and the driver, Gino, took us to the boat ramp to unload our bags, then drove us up to the campground where we'd stored our boats.

"How much for the ride, Gino?" I asked.

"Eleven dollars."

I paused. "How much?" I was surprised. Gino had driven to the DoubleTree, taken us six miles to the marina, then to the campground.

"Eleven dollars."

VO gave Gino a twenty and told him to keep the change. Gino must have said thank you half a dozen times.

We started with a slight tailwind out of the southwest. Calm morning. Cool temps. We paddled past downtown Maysville, then past the charming river town of Ripley, Ohio.

Then the wind picked up.

My WillyWeather app was showing winds out of the west-southwest at 12 miles an hour, gusting to 20. And around noon, we got the full force of that 20 miles an hour. Head on.

Whitecaps. Steady waves. I was paddling but barely moving. One mile an hour at best. VO in his kayak seemed to love the waves, but I really had to work to make any progress—and keep from being hit broadside by the waves and tipping over.

There is almost nothing worse on the river than pulling hard with every stroke, shoulders burning, and seeing the shoreline barely creeping past.

I wasn't having any fun at all. 1 p.m. came and went. Then 2, then 3.

At 3:15, we finally made it to Augusta, Kentucky. I thought back on the day. From 8:45 to noon, we had paddled 14 miles, but in the same amount of time, from noon to 3:15, we had paddled 6.

I wanted to stop in Augusta. Cute park. Picnic tables. 20 miles for the day. But VO clearly wanted to keep going. If it had been an hour later in the day, I would've called a halt. But it was only 3:15, so off we went, back into battling the waves.

We paddled past Augusta, which really was a cute riverside town. Then we paddled around a small car ferry being pushed by a tug that was going back and forth between Augusta and the Ohio side of the river. After that, we drifted past an authentic paddlewheeler that looked like it had come from Cincinnati, stopped in Augusta for a couple of hours, and was now heading back to Cincinnati. All this commotion, along with the twenty-mile-an-hour wind, really churned up the water.

It was a bit scary as two-foot waves crashed into my little canoe from every direction. I stayed focused and powered through the maelstrom, turning my bow back and forth to try to hit the next wave head on and keep from taking one over the side and getting swamped.

Scary and exhausting. It only made me madder that we hadn't stopped at the park in Augusta.

We pushed into the wind and waves for two more miles, just creeping along, and finally paddled up Turtle Creek until we found a passable camping spot. Just big enough for two tents. We had to climb up a steep, muddy bank, beat down tall grass, and move some branches out of the way. But we were done for the day. Home for the night.

Two and a half days from our halfway point, in terms of both mileage and time.

The wind seemed to be dying down, the terrifying waves from a couple of hours ago now only a memory.

VO and I clinked glasses. The bourbon had smoothed the rough edges of the day.

DAY 21

October 7, 2024

Turtle Creek to New Richmond, OH

21 miles
Total: 450 miles

Towns and locks: Captain Anthony Meldahl Lock and Dam (436), New Richmond (450)

Billy—not his real name—had been trying to convince us there was no such thing as an undertow in the ocean. Now he was telling us a story about flying to Myrtle Beach, somehow tying this to our previous topic of airplane pilots experiencing spatial disorientation.

"So the pilot says, 'Get ready to ditch it in the river!'" Billy droned on, but I'd stopped listening a while ago.

We were sitting on the front porch of a large, late-1800s brick home on the shores of the Ohio River in New Richmond, Ohio. Bob—also not his real name, and more on him later—was also on the porch with us, along with a very large man wearing camo shorts and sucking on a lollipop, and an older African American man with a fishing pole. Lollipop guy was now telling a story about seeing Bigfoot during a turkey-hunting trip he was on. True story.

Billy was still talking. "... and that's not even a fishing pole," he said, pointing to the guy with the fishing pole. "It's a wand to ward off evil spirits ..." True story.

How did we end up in this scene right out of a Far Side comic strip? I wondered, just as Billy broke into a rendition of "Ol' Man River."

I mentally went over our day, which had started at our little camp in the trees. Deer had been stomping past our tents last night, and at least three trains had roared past us, loud as heck. The ground shook, we were so close to the tracks.

At least our tents were dry this morning. No fog, and almost no dew.

We were on the river by 8:45 a.m. It was fifty degrees and chilly, but sunny, and the wind was only two to three miles an hour out of the north. Really nice paddling weather.

Around mile 3, the wind started to pick up, and within minutes, it was blowing ten to fifteen miles an hour—and gusting even higher—straight out of the north, and we were paddling due north.

All. Day. Long.

It was an intense, grueling paddle. Just inching along.

Whitecaps.

It was frustrating paddling in nonstop wind. A beautiful day, other than the wind.

(Billy had not stopped talking. Bob just went off to bed, leaving us with the rest of the porch-sitting crazies.)

We'd planned on paddling 24–25 miles today, but after a couple of hours of paddling into the wind and waves, I knew we wouldn't get anywhere near that far.

By 2 p.m., we'd traveled 12 miles, averaging around two miles an hour. VO and I agreed we'd keep going for another three hours, until 5:00.

It was a long three hours.

Around 4 p.m., we decided to cross from the Kentucky side of the river to the Ohio side. I was apprehensive because of the whitecaps, but I went for it.

About two hundred yards into it, maybe a quarter of the way across, I started wishing that I hadn't started for the other side. Two- to three-foot waves, one right after the other, crashed over my bow. Soon, I had water sloshing around inside my boat, which greatly reduced the stability of my canoe.

(Billy was now talking about the winter the Ohio River had frozen over. I didn't believe him, so I Googled it, and sure enough, it had frozen over in 1994. I wondered if that meant the rest of the things he'd said were true as well?)

After the exhausting, nerve-wracking paddle to the other side, I was very relieved to have made it across.

Now we were nearing New Richmond, a charming river town, that stretched about a mile and a half along the Ohio side of the river. The map showed a boat ramp about two miles from the start of town. That was our goal, to make it to that boat ramp. We could probably be there by 5:30 p.m.

Just as we passed the first couple of houses, I noticed a man, a woman, and a tiny dog out on a dock. They yelled hello as I approached, so I paddled closer.

The man was Bob and the woman was his neighbor. I told them about our Ohio River thru-paddle and asked if it was possible to camp right there at the boat ramp.

"You guys can set up your tents in my front yard," Bob said. "I have a bathroom and laundry you can use. Heck, I'll even take you guys out to dinner tonight."

I graciously accepted the offer without conferring with VO, who was a few minutes behind me. We'd only paddled twenty-one miles, but sleeping on someone's lawn and going out to dinner would offer way better stories than paddling two more miles into the wind and getting kicked out by the local police for trying to camp at a public boat ramp.

Little did I know.

Bob lived in a big, brick house just two hundred yards downriver from where he'd said hello, so VO and I paddled off and pulled out near the house as Bob walked down to greet us. We hauled our boats and gear a ways up the shore, then cable-locked our boats together. Eighty-year-old Bob even helped us haul three loads of packs and dry bags up the steps and across the street to his front yard.

(The large guy sitting on the porch with us was named Marshal. "They used to call me Dopey Marshal," said Marshal, "because I was all fucked up back then. Part of a motorcycle gang.")

From the moment we stepped ashore, Bob had been telling stories. He was a retired corporate jet pilot and had been the private pilot for a famous Formula One racecar driver. He had also managed an airport for Hugh Hefner. Bob was an airplane junky, and as such, made airplane references all night long.

A self-proclaimed historian, philosopher, and amateur sociologist, Bob was very interested in people and why they did what they did. He was also a gifted storyteller—in the sense that he never stopped talking—and Billy, who had turned out to be Bob's brother, was not to be outdone.

("You guys are shantyboaters," Billy was saying to us. "Shantyboaters live on the river. They just drift down the river, looking for a better life. Did you know that back in the day, the first two rows of corn or vegetables grown in a garden were reserved for the shantyboaters?" He kept going.)

We carried our stuff up to the big, red-brick house, where a humongous Trump flag flew from the porch, and a Trump sign stood proudly in the yard.

"I saw the 'Harris for President' sticker on your boat," Bob said. "Do you want me to take down my Trump sign for the night so that you're more comfortable camping in my yard?" He would have done it.

I chuckled. "No way. I can't wait to send my wife a photo of my tent next to a Trump yard sign!"

(Another guy, Chaco, just showed up on the porch. Apparently he lived here, too.)

We set up our tents, then I went inside with Bob so he could show me where the bathroom was. There were cats and dogs *everywhere*, and I had to squeeze between massive piles of junk to make my way down the hallway. The place smelled terrible.

"When you come in to use the bathroom," Bob said, "bring a flashlight. The light switch doesn't work. And there's no hot water in the tub." As I poked my head inside the bathroom, a horrendous stench hit me, and I had to hold my breath. Then, in the dim light of the bathroom, I saw it.

The toilet was completely full of shit. *Full*.

The longer I sat on Bob's porch tonight, listening to Chaco, Marshal, and Billy, the weirder this place got. The Eagles song "Hotel California" kept running through my mind. There was something very strange going on here. Bob owned this house, the huge house next door, three other houses in town, a house two hours from here, and a commercial property somewhere (according to him anyway). Yet the lights in this house didn't even work, and the toilet in the main bathroom was clogged with crap.

Then Marshal told us something even weirder: the house next door, which Bob rented out, had no power and no running water.

Rented out? I couldn't believe it.

I had a feeling there was something unspoken going on around here, and it was starting to creep me out. Bob, who had allegedly been a private pilot for most of his career, was now a slumlord.

Earlier, after he had offered to take VO and me out to dinner, we drove to a Mexican restaurant in his totally rusted-out and beat-up car. VO and I ended up paying for the whole thing once we realized Bob wasn't ever going to reach for his wallet.

Bob had also offered to take us to McDonald's tomorrow morning at 7:30 for breakfast and coffee before we got back on the river. We'd go, but then we planned to pack up and get the heck out of here, and it wouldn't be soon enough.

I reflected on our cast of characters:

BILLY

This was Bob's younger brother who actually looked older. He was funny, but very odd, and was constantly breaking out in song. Nonstop chatter. Full of incredible stories and crazy theories. Completely dependent on his older brother. A couple of years ago, he had been renting one of Bob's other homes and had run short on money. After his brother evicted him, he moved into this house with Bob, completely dependent on him to this day.

CHACO

Hispanic guy who spoke almost no English. Bob had taken him in, too. He worked at a local restaurant and kept his car parked in the middle of the front yard. When Bob had first brought me into the house earlier today, he pointed to a large dog bed amongst the clutter on the living room floor and said, "That's where Chaco sleeps." I thought Chaco was one of the many dogs roaming around the house, until we actually met him. When we were setting up our tents earlier this evening, Billy came out with three big orange traffic cones and set them up around our tents, like a perimeter. Sensing our confusion, he explained he didn't want Chaco to run us over in his car when he got home tonight. That didn't make sense until we saw Chaco drive across the yard and park on the lawn by the front porch.

MARSHAL

Big guy who worked for thirty years as a laborer, got involved in a motorcycle gang, became an alcoholic, and spent time in and out of jail for fighting. Bob was good friends with the local judge, who said he would only let Marshal off on bail if Bob provided him with a place to sleep. Bob claimed Marshal was mentally ill, but I thought Marshal came across as the most normal guy in the bunch. Later in the evening, Marshal told us that Bob was "an evil and horrible man. I could tell you lots of horrible stories about him."

JAMES

African American man who lived here, too. James carried around a fishing pole with a small flashlight tied to the top and went from house to house casting out evil spirits.

They all lived in this house with Bob, and they were all completely dependent on him. In a weird way, by the things Bob said and did, he seemed to be proving his superiority over them. And they all lived in a mansion that stunk of shit. Later, VO reported that the toilet in the downstairs bathroom was also full of shit. Everything was filthy.

What the hell was going on here?

DAY 22

October 8, 2024

New Richmond, OH, to the Ludlow Bromley marina

24 miles
Total: 474 miles

Town and locks: Newport (470), Cincinnati (471), Bromley (474)

We paddled through downtown Cincinnati today, which was pretty cool. Not only was getting to Cincinnati a long-awaited, long-anticipated milestone for this river trip, but it was the first of several other milestones we hit today.

We'll reach the halfway point on the Ohio River tomorrow, and if we make it 26 miles before quitting time today, which isn't likely, we'll even hit the 500-mile mark of our trip.

The river took several twists and turns as it approached Cincinnati. There were at least six major bends in the river, so there was something new around every corner. On a long river trip, where I'm in my boat pretty much all day long, any diversion for my mind helps, including bends in the river.

We paddled right past the Reds baseball stadium and the Bengals football stadium, where lots of people were walking along the river. We also paddled under six bridges as we made our way past Cincinnati. There was a lot to look at, and these distractions made the miles pass quickly.

The day had been almost perfect. It was only forty-four degrees when we crawled out of our soaking-wet tents a little after 7 a.m., feeling glad we hadn't been run over by Chaco—or worse. We were glad to be paddling away from that big brick house by 9, pushing off in a heavy, moist fog. It took about an hour for the fog to burn off, and then it was relatively cool and cloudless for the rest of the day.

There was a light breeze out of the north. The first eight miles zipped by in just two hours. Four miles an hour on this river was moving pretty fast. I was on the phone for a good part of the morning with Seth, Leslie, and my mom, so the time and miles flew by.

We'd paddled past quite a few marinas with riverside restaurants over the last couple of days as we got closer to Cincinnati. I remembered seeing a lot of these on my Mississippi and Tennessee River trips, but we'd passed very few on the Ohio River so far. We didn't stop at any of them, but I hoped we'd start seeing more as we paddled along the southern border of Indiana.

Over the past day, two people had told us the high hills we'd been seeing on both sides of the river, pretty much since the start of the trip, would mellow out and the shorelines would be flatter. I hoped that meant we'd pass more river towns and marinas in the coming weeks.

Even though it only got up to seventy-one degrees today, being on the water fried my nose and cheeks.

Just after 4 p.m., we paddled up to the Ludlow Bromley Marina. We wanted a place to safely stow our boats so we could get a hotel in or near Cincinnati, and this marina was the last spot I could see on the map for the next several miles.

Steve, the marina manager, said we were welcome to pull our boats and gear up onto the shore for the night. He told us a story of a fifteen-barge tow that had smashed into this marina four years ago, taking out most of the docks and slips, and wiping out the floating restaurant. According to Steve, both the tug captain and the entire crew had fallen asleep and missed a turn in the river. We could still see a lot of damage that hadn't been repaired yet. Steve said it would still be another year before everything was rebuilt.

We called an Uber to take us to an extended stay hotel in Covington, Kentucky, then stood along the road and waited forty minutes for it to show up. During most of that time, we were talking to a retired—

and very curious—local from Ludlow, where the marina was. His name was Dave, and he had been out for a walk when he saw us. He stopped to pepper us with questions:

- Where are you from?
- Do you have jobs?
- How has retirement been going (for VO)?
- Is Sitka, Alaska (where I used to live) mostly a rain forest?
- How long is your boat?
- Do you guys camp?
- What has the river been like?
- Have kids been throwing stones at you from the shore? (Not sure where Dave got that idea.)

Our hotel was just across a bridge from downtown Cincinnati and a couple of blocks from the main street of Covington, which had dozens of cute bars and restaurants. A cool spot that would be fun to come back to sometime. We found a bar and sat outside. VO and I both got IPAs that had come from the 3 Floyds brewery in Indiana, one of my favorite breweries. The beer helped wash down the huge Greek gyro pizza.

So, a little more about our host last night, Bob ...

Bob met us outside our tents this morning at 7:30 and drove us to McDonald's for breakfast. Super nice.

He pointed out various houses and places of interest along the way, including the Cardboard Boat Museum in New Richmond. He seemed thrilled to be talking with us. Eager for the "intellectual stimulation," as he called it.

"You know, I don't understand why it's a problem that these adult female teachers are having sex with teenage boys," he said out of the blue while we downed our Egg McMuffins. "Why is that a problem? It's good for those boys. It's what they need."

VO the pediatrician perked up. "Would you think differently if it was a male teacher and teenage girls?"

"Well, of course. That's different. But it's just the way boys are wired."

One of Marshal's allegations against Bob last night had been that he was running a teen sex ring, so now I was hyper alert to everything Bob was saying.

"Bob," I said, "there are lots of other things going on in terms of power and control, like an adult being in a power relationship over a child. We need laws that set age limits around certain behaviors."

Bob ignored my comment and continued talking nonstop and pontificating on an array of topics. But once it was clear we didn't agree with him on a certain topic, he'd drop it and move on, like he was baiting us to see what we'd agree with.

"You know, when a little five-year-old dies," he said (after I told him VO was a pediatrician), "it makes the rest of the human race stronger. People, and even children, need to die to make society stronger and help it flourish."

What the fuck?

Bob also talked about how much he loved his mother as a child and how he'd been totally in love with his mom's breasts. He was telling two total strangers that he loved his mom's big breasts.

This seemed to be Bob's overarching theme: since we are all driven by nature, there's really no such thing as personal responsibility. Female teachers are drawn to young boys. That's nature. Criminals and deviants are born that way and don't really have a choice. That's genetic. Crime, premature death, and war atrocities are all necessary because it ultimately makes the human race stronger.

After thinking more about Bob while I paddled today, I concluded that between his glee in describing his mom's big, beautiful breasts, his support of adult women having sex with boys, and Marshal's allegation of "teen sex slaves," he was a really sick puppy. Super intelligent, to the point where he felt superior to the people he let stay in his house, referring to his brother Billy as "uneducated" and to Marshal as "mentally ill," but in the end, he was just the overlord of a small, dysfunctional kingdom.

VO and I learned and surmised all of this in just twelve hours. And I don't think we had even scratched the surface of all the weird and twisted things going on in that household.

Our stay in New Richmond had been like an episode of a true crime podcast.

Sharing the Ohio River with the Belle of Cincinnati paddleboat

This gracious yard owner asked if he should take his Trump sign down when he saw the Harris sticker on my canoe

Downtown Cincinnati

Wildlife on the Ohio River

Old river dredge just outside of Cincinnati, Day 22

We paddled past several coal-powered electricity plants

Starting to get chilly, October 10 (Day 24)

More fog paddling out of Warsaw, Kentucky, Day 25

Camping just a few inches above the waterline made me nervous, Day 26

VO's wife, Val, helping to get his boat in the water on Day 28 near Louisville, Kentucky

Counting the bridges leading out of Louisville

Paddling in the rain on Day 29

Downtown Louisville

My second-favorite whiskey of the trip, with some camping hors d'oeuvres

Kent, owner of The Dock restaurant in Leavenworth, Indiana, went out of his way to help us

Smith Holler Distillery in Cloverport, Kentucky, Day 33

No better place to be

Candy, the mayor of Cloverport, Kentucky, let us camp at the boat ramp park

No words

Keith and Anna travel to meet us in Troy, Indiana

A beach fire: the perfect end to a long paddle, Day 38

A tug and barges pass us near Henderson, Kentucky

Low river levels mean no current to help us along

Almost November and the leaves are starting to turn

River angels welcome us in Paducah, Kentucky, on Day 43

Portaging across a cornfield

Two farm boys, Blake and Josh, offer to help us portage our boats

Our last campfire, Day 45

Perfect way to end our adventure

Jeff joins us to paddle the final ten miles on our last day

Perfect weather on our last day

Fort Defiance State Park with the Mississippi River in the distance

Celebrating mile 981 with VO and Monkey Face

The end

DAY 23

October 9, 2024

Ludlow Bromley marina to Lighthouse Point marina (past Aurora, IN)

25 miles
Total: 499 miles

Towns and locks: Anderson Ferry crossing (477½), halfway point on the Ohio River (490½), Lawrenceburg (493½), Aurora (497)

Today was a big day in terms of trip milestones.

Mile 16½ was our official halfway point on the Ohio River: 490½ miles! We stopped paddling in the middle of the river and shot a short celebration video to send to our family supporters.

At mile 17½ for the day, we paddled past the Little Miami River, which formed the border between Ohio and Indiana. We had officially passed into Indiana on the right bank, but we still had Kentucky on the left.

We stopped for the night at river mile 499, meaning that first thing tomorrow we'd pass 500 miles. Lots of evidence that we were making progress, but we still had a long way to go.

It's 5:30 p.m., and we're sitting in our camp chairs along the riverbank, enjoying a glass of 1792 whiskey. We have a great campsite, as long as we don't get kicked out—a nice grassy, shaded spot right on the river. It's the private property of the Lighthouse Point marina, but we're over a hill and out of sight, so hopefully no one will see us down here and ask us to leave.

I'd been feeling exceptionally tired all day, and the whiskey wasn't helping. We didn't turn out our hotel lights last night until 10:30, after I had finished a work video call, packed up our clean laundry, done some computer work, and read a bit. Up by 6 a.m. and at Waffle House for breakfast by 7, so not as much sleep as I'd been getting, since we typically crawled into our tents by 7:30 p.m.

It was peaceful now. No breeze. The river was calm. A relaxing moment of no movement, other than occasionally lifting my whiskey glass to my mouth.

I miss home. I miss Leslie. I miss Seth and Shauna and my grandsons, Arlo and Rio. I miss Tyler and Dana and baby Coletta. We've been on the river for twenty-three days now. That is a long time. Maybe in another week I'll feel like we are getting closer to being home, but right now, Cairo, Illinois, is still a long, long ways away.

If we average 23 miles a day, we'll be done by October 30. Averaging 25 miles a day gets us done only one day sooner. But that seems overly optimistic since we've never paddled more than 25 miles and sometimes don't even hit 23 with wind and waves. And these predictions don't include taking any days off for weather or rest.

So October 30 is now the goal. Today is October 9, which means we have three more weeks on the river. What a great opportunity, something that other people only dream about: being able to paddle down a river for three full weeks.

My ninety-two-year-old mom was telling me on the phone today how, in the midst of Israel's war in Gaza and Russia's war against Ukraine, and with Hurricane Milton about to reach landfall tonight with Tampa in the crosshairs, just after the devastation of Hurricane Helene two weeks ago, and among so many other horrible events, our job as people on this earth is to do something good to help others in each of our own little spheres of influence. In our own little worlds.

And if we all just do that—find a way to make someone smile—then we'll be helping to make the world just a little better place today. My mom told me about two interactions she and her dog Bella had had today, both with strangers, that made her smile. And made me smile. In her very important way, she made the world a better place today.

It was now 7:15 p.m., and while VO and I were sitting in our camp chairs sipping whiskey, and I was writing in my journal, a big, fancy, black pickup pulled up next to our tents, driven by a guy who wasn't smiling. I got up and walked over and shook his hand. His name was Mark. He asked us what we thought we were doing on private property. Apparently, he owned the marina and wasn't happy that we were camped on his property. Then a woman drove up on her tractor pulling a grass mower. This was Sandy. She'd seen us when she was mowing earlier and had called Mark.

We explained our trip, and Mark seemed impressed, but he wanted to see our boats as proof before he'd believe our story. So we walked the few hundred yards back to where we'd pulled our boats out of the water. He had thought we were either homeless—the horror—or doing drugs.

VO immediately offered Mark and Sandy some whiskey, which they both readily said yes to, and we ended up having a nice chat. Mark ended up being super friendly.

Sandy was a hoot. She'd driven heavy equipment and dump trucks her entire life and was currently cutting Mark's sprawling acreage of grass. She also raced a 4x4 Jeep. Brown, leathery skin. Tank top. Swore like a sailor.

The four of us stood around drinking whiskey. Shooting the shit. It turned out to be awesome. Sandy offered to let us take showers and do our laundry up at the marina. And top off our water jugs.

Sandy had more grass to cut, so she eventually got back on her tractor and drove off. Mark stayed and talked for a while. Sandy called Mark while we were still talking and offered to pick us up a pizza and bring it down. She also offered to grab clean towels for the shower. Then Mark offered to drive us up to the bathrooms that were about half a mile away. All of which we declined. It was already past our bedtimes, and we had just showered and done laundry last night. But they were very nice offers. Two people who had started out very suspicious and ended up being really friendly.

Mark told us that when Sandy first spotted us, she had called him and said, "I've got two guns. Want me to bring 'em down and confront those guys?"

Thankfully, Mark said no to that.

Sandy and Mark. I still remember the combination to the marina bathroom: 2133.

DAY 24

October 10, 2024

Lighthouse Point marina to Warsaw, KY

29 miles
Total: 528 miles

Towns and locks: Rising Sun (506), Patriot (519), Warsaw (528)

Last night at 9:00, VO and I were all buttoned up in our tents and camped at the marina, when bright lights came toward us. A truck engine shuddered to a stop.

"Hey, you boys!" a woman yelled. "I brought you a hot dinner!"

It was Sandy.

Despite our having declined her offer to get us pizza a couple of hours ago, she was back with a medium pepperoni pizza from Domino's, along with paper plates and napkins.

"Now, eat up," she said. "I know how much a good hot meal can make a difference. And you boys make sure to get a hot shower in the morning, too."

Sandy. What an amazing person.

Chain-smoking, tractor-driving, gun-toting Sandy.

VO and I each ate one obligatory piece of pizza and saved the rest for the next day.

It got down to forty-three degrees overnight, and it was dark and still chilly at 7 a.m. when I started packing up inside my tent. But by 7:30, there was plenty of light to fire up my stove and boil water for oatmeal and coffee. I hesitated for a minute or two, half expecting Sandy to show up with hot grits and gravy.

She didn't, so I threw on my hooded sweatshirt and my windbreaker—and short pants, of course—to stay warm while I ate my oatmeal with Craisins.

There was a nice breeze, and it was blowing our way, south. This was the first morning of the last twenty-four days that we had woken up to a favorable wind.

For the first couple of hours, we had a four- or five-mile-an hour tailwind. Steam rose from the river as the cold air met the warmer water, which made the sunrise and our morning paddle especially beautiful.

But I could feel right away this morning that paddling all day was going to be a chore for me. I just wasn't into it. After paddling for what seemed like forever, I checked the map on my phone. We'd only gone three and a half miles. I usually make a point of not looking at my watch or checking the map very often, especially in the morning, because it can really drag out the miles.

Around mile 5, the wind switched direction and started blowing into our faces. I also typically don't turn on my AM/FM radio or listen to music on my iPhone until we've been paddling for a few hours. I use those as a reward or save them for distractions on days when my mind is struggling or the miles are just creeping by.

But this morning, I turned my radio on right away and thankfully found a public radio station with BBC News, local news, and the 1A news talk show. There was plenty of Hurricane Milton news: storm surges, flooding, death.

I had my earbuds in and was listening to music by mile 10. The day just seemed to stretch out for me, and the miles came slowly.

Just one of those days.

Music got me through the afternoon: Queen, Patti Griffin, James Taylor, U2. Then, when I really needed a jolt of motivation, Dropkick Murphys with my favorite song, "Smash Shit Up."

We paddled toward the spot at mile 24 I'd picked out to stop at. But it was only 3:30 p.m. and that was too early to stop, even for me. So we paddled on. I told VO I didn't want to paddle much past 4:30. That would be eight hours of paddling with only two very short stops all day long.

Around 4:15, we started watching for a level spot that would be big enough to set up two tents, but there was nothing. We paddled past several small weekend cottages and mobile homes, hoping to see a car or someone outside we could ask for permission to set up our tents. But nothing.

Mile 25.

Mile 26.

Mile 27.

Nothing.

Then we spotted what looked like a boat ramp across the river and paddled over to it.

It turned out to be private property that led up to a beautiful mansion on the riverbank: the Riverside Inn bed and breakfast. I thought I might as well call them since we were floating literally down below their front door.

$279 a night. It was too fancy for us anyway.

It looked beautiful, but we decided to paddle on. We found a city park and boat ramp at mile 29, and Google maps showed a campground at mile 31. We stopped at the city park and finally got out of our boats at 5:30 p.m. Long day!

We pulled our boats out of the water, and VO went to chat it up with an older couple sitting in their pickup truck near the river. I called the Warsaw, Kentucky, city office (closed) then rang the mayor's office (no answer).

The last thing we wanted to do after a long day of paddling was set up, go to sleep, then get kicked out by the local police in the middle of the night.

At the park restroom I met Joe, a city worker who was locking up the bathrooms for the night.

"Sure," he said, "you can camp here. No problem."

"But the sign says the park is closed from dusk to dawn."

"Don't worry about it. People camp down here all the time. There was a guy camped down here for two weeks a while back."

“That’s the best thing you could’ve said,” I told him, hardly hiding my elation. “We’ve been paddling for nine straight hours today.”

“I’ll run by the police station and let them know you’re here. Have fun. Build yourselves a fire. There’s plenty of driftwood down there.”

Welcome to Warsaw, Kentucky.

VO’s older couple concurred that camping would not be a problem. They also said we should eat two blocks up the street at Jewell’s on Main. So, after we got set up and stowed our gear, we walked to Jewell’s for dinner.

Carrie, who took our order, came over and pulled up a chair to sit with VO and me while we ate our meals. “So, what are you guys doing?” she asked, seeing our journals open on the table. It must have looked a little weird.

Super friendly with a cute personality. She had great tattoos on one of her arms from her eight mission trips to Haiti.

Carrie told us there were two-hundred–pound catfish in the river. And that a bobcat had recently been spotted in town. She also hoped we hadn’t caught any diseases from paddling the river.

I reminded her that we were in boats, not swimming.

“Well, I wouldn’t let that water touch you,” Carrie said. “Some of those catfish have four or five eyes.”

DAY 25

October 11, 2024

Warsaw, KY, to (almost) Brooksburg, IN

22 miles
Total: 550 miles

Towns and locks: Florence (529), Belterra Casino Resort (530), Markland Lock and Dam (531½), Vevay (538), Carrollton (545)

Holy ... ! What a day!

It's always so nice to be done. All our cares and hardships melt away, and then they just become part of the story. Everything we do just becomes part of a story in the end. A story that, honestly, most people wouldn't be interested in hearing. A story most people couldn't ever relate to. But paddling the Ohio River is part of my story.

I'd been waking up before 6 every morning on this trip, but today, it wasn't until after 6 that I crawled out of my tent, which was soaked in dew from the heavy fog. We were camped next to a covered shelter with picnic tables, which gave me a dry place to sit and drink my instant Starbucks. It was only forty-two degrees, so I wore my fleece hat and draped my down blanket over my legs. I checked emails and did some work on my laptop until the sun started to come up around 7. Then I walked over to rouse VO.

While I sat at the picnic table typing with my frozen fingers, a guy pulled up in his pickup truck: a city worker checking on some broken lighting. He told me about the West Side Diner, a breakfast place just three blocks away. It opened at 6 a.m., he said, and the food was fantastic. "It's kind of pricey, though. Like, ten dollars. But worth it."

The second VO was out of his tent, we walked over to the West Side

Diner and had a huge breakfast, which included the weakest coffee I'd ever had. But the coffee mug was warm. And the people were friendly. And it beat the hell out of eating oatmeal in the cold fog at our picnic table.

The fog was still heavy as we packed up our boats. Everything was wet. The air was cold. I waited to take off until VO was ready because the fog was too thick to paddle more than about twenty-five yards from each other.

There were hundreds of submerged branches and trees and logs all along the left side of the river. I scraped over the top of a few of the bigger ones. A huge log that was barely below the surface almost tipped me over. I had to strike the balance of paddling far enough offshore to miss the submerged logs, but close enough not to lose sight of the shore. As we'd learned, there were tugs with barges that still moved up and down the river in thick fog.

The Markland Lock and Dam was at mile 3½ for the day. We paddled right up to the large, concrete sidewalls before we ever saw the massive dam. I called the lockmaster and he said the big chamber was under repair. When we arrived, they were breaking down a 1,200-foot–long tow into 600-foot sections to lock the barges through. He told us it would be at least a three-hour wait.

I asked the lockmaster about portaging around. He described a boat ramp on the left bank and said we would have to haul our stuff about three-quarters of a mile to the downriver side of the dam. That sounded better than waiting three hours, and it was still early in the morning, so we pulled over at an unused concrete boat ramp that was so littered with logs, branches, and rocks that we couldn't even use our boat trailers.

It took several trips to haul up our bags and boats while scrambling over dozens of drift logs. The steep ramp led to a busy road where we put our boats on their two-wheeled trailers, loaded them again, and dragged them down the side of the road to the entrance of the lock parking lot.

I wasn't sure if we could enter the signed "Private Federal Property" area, so I left my boat on the sidewalk along the busy road and walked around until I found an Army Corps employee. I asked him where we could put our boats back in. He told me to continue along the main road, cross over a bridge, then head down a little side creek that would take us back to the Ohio River.

Easy enough.

We pulled our boats another quarter mile to the bridge. I walked ahead of VO and looked down over the railing. There was almost no water in the creek.

I turned around and gave VO a thumbs-down.

The Army Corps employee also said he'd seen cars parked on the side of the road, just past the bridge, where people walked down to the Ohio River to fish.

We dragged our heavy loads another few hundred yards and found the trail he was talking about. Pulling these heavily loaded boats on two tiny wheels with over a hundred pounds of gear was tiring, especially pulling them uphill.

There was a concrete barrier across the front of the trail, probably to keep four-wheelers out. I grabbed several of my bags and started down the trail to scout it out, which left my canoe a little lighter for the second trip down.

The trail ended up being a good half mile long. Several downed trees crisscrossed the path, and we had to duck under a few more. I took the time to locate a few side trails that avoided most of the fallen trees.

The trail ended at the top of a small, rocky ridge that led a hundred yards down through rocks and boulders to the river.

One load done.

Back to get our boats and the rest of our gear.

Pulling the now half-loaded boats along the trail was a little more challenging. We had to help each other lift our boats over the trees that had fallen across the trail.

We had started portaging at 10 a.m., and by noon we had everything loaded back up and we were ready to paddle. The tug that had been ahead of us in the lock was now getting ready to push his last few barges into the lock. We'd picked the quicker option, but also the more exhausting one.

Three hours since shoving off this morning and we'd only managed to go three and a half miles. An inauspicious start.

It was a beautiful day today. Sunny. Cloudless. High around seventy-five. But shortly after we started paddling again, a breeze kicked in, and for the rest of the day we were paddling into a five- to seven-mile-an-hour headwind. It made for a long and exhausting day.

I suggested to VO that we plan to be done by 5 p.m. regardless of how far we'd paddled, and that we start looking for a camping spot after 4:30. He seemed fine with that, so we paddled on. Listening to music got me through the day once again.

The only town of any size we paddled past was Carrollton, Kentucky.

When we took a break around 3 p.m., I thought we'd logged 16 miles, but it was really only 14. We eventually paddled past an RV park at mile 20. By now, it was already after 5:00. We got out and wandered around until we found a guy to ask if we could set up our tents somewhere out of the way. He told us we should ask the owners and pointed to a house that was half a mile away.

Screw it.

We got back into our boats and headed to another RV park, keeping our eyes peeled for any possible spots to camp along the riverbank. But there just weren't any level spots.

We pulled off again at 5:45 down below some trailers that were parked up on a hill. Two young guys were pulling an aluminum canoe down the trailer park boat ramp. The canoe was balanced on a skateboard so they could roll it down the ramp.

Brilliant.

One of the guys, Chase, had just moved to this RV park from Maine. He told us everyone living here was "chill" and said we could definitely camp for the night. "If anyone tries to kick you out, just tell them Chase said it was okay."

Twenty minutes later, after we'd hauled all our gear up the hill and were setting up our tents, a guy in a golf cart pulled up and asked what we thought we were doing.

"Chase said it would be okay," I replied. "We—" Then it dawned on me. "Chase didn't have any authority to tell us that, did he?"

"No, sir."

We told him our paddling-the-Ohio-River story, after which he introduced himself as Rod and said we could stay—as long as we didn't break the law.

Whatever that meant.

Anyway, VO and I were too exhausted to break any laws at that point.

Black beans, rice, tortillas, whiskey, and a chocolate bar. Sitting in our chairs overlooking the Ohio River. Not a bad end to a long day.

DAY 26

October 12, 2024

Brooksburg, IN, to river mile 571

21 miles
Total: 571 miles

Towns and locks: Brooksburg (551), Madison/Milton (557)

At 4:00 this afternoon, I boiled over.

From 9 a.m. until noon, we'd had perfect weather and flat, calm water. No tailwind and still no current, but otherwise perfect. I even got to FaceTime my grandsons, Arlo and Rio. But right after noon, the wind kicked up and blew ten to fifteen miles an hour for the rest of the day.

We crossed the river twice to shorten the distance of the bends, and both times I cursed myself for agreeing to cross with the wind and waves that came up over my bow while out in the middle.

When paddling in waves, you either have to take them head on or at a forty-five–degree angle, quartering the waves to make sure they don't come over the side and swamp your canoe. It requires concentration and constant vigilance. And in my thirteen-and-a-half-foot–long canoe, which was loaded with 220 pounds—me and about 100 pounds of gear and food—I sit pretty low in the water. So it doesn't take much to get a wave over the side.

By 4 p.m., I'd had enough.

We still had 4 miles to go to our 25-mile goal, where there was a boat ramp and a cluster of houses called Bethlehem, Indiana. For a while, I'd been asking myself why we were always pushing ourselves to get 25 miles in every day. Why did we always wait until 5 p.m. before looking for a place to camp? Why not, say, 4 p.m.? After we'd unloaded our boats, set up camp, cooked dinner, and journaled by the light of our headlamps, it would be time for bed. Was a campfire and a little extra daylight too much to ask?

VO had stopped and was waiting for me before we crossed—*again*—to the other side of the river, and I just let it all out.

"You know, in the last twenty-five days," I said, "we've only had *one* campfire. Mostly because we're always too tired to look for wood. We've only stopped in *one* town while paddling during the day, and that was at 4 p.m. And even then, instead of camping there, we just grabbed a beer and food to go and kept on paddling into the wind for another two hours and ended up at a horrible camping spot! Why are we doing this to ourselves?"

The past few days hadn't been much fun for me, I told VO, and I wanted to dial it back a little bit. We had too many days left on this trip to keep pushing so hard every single day. It had been giving me feelings of dread every morning as I lay in bed. If we only had 4 or 5 days left, sure, go balls to the wall and get it done. But with 17 days left? I wanted to take it a little easier some days and only paddle 7 hours instead of 8 or 9.

When I FaceTimed Seth today, he reminded me to enjoy the moments, the Zen moments of paddling. And to take in the scenery. To appreciate the experience. He is always good at helping me slow down and be more centered. Seth planted the seed earlier today to call myself out, pull back on our hard-ass pace, and find ways to build in more enjoyment.

Sitting by the fire for the last hour and a half has been immensely satisfying. The ground we are camping on is low, rocky, and kind of muddy. We had to look around to find a couple of tent spots. But a roaring fire seemed to make even the junkiest camping spot feel like home.

Finding a balance between pushing hard enough to accomplish a goal—in this case, thru-paddling all 981 miles of the Ohio River—and also finding ways to have fun is a challenge. Paddling 10–15 miles a day, which would be awesome, would allow us to stop in just about every town, but would turn this into an eighty- to ninety-day trip. That is waaaaay longer than I want to be gone. But the flipside, trying to hit 25 miles every day with no current and steady wind in our faces, was mostly no fun.

I knew there was something in the middle. And that middle is different for every person, every trip, every day. Somewhere in the middle was the "sweet spot," as paddling guru Park Neff used to say.

DAY 27

October 13, 2024

River mile 571 to Westport, KY

9½ miles
Total: 580½ miles

Towns and locks: Bethlehem (575), Westport (580½)

Today, the river slapped us upside our heads.

"Taking what the river gives you is such an easy thing to say!" I shouted to VO as we battled a 20–25-mile-an-hour headwind and two-and-a-half-foot waves, echoing what my paddling cousin Jeff often said. "But that's hard for me to integrate into my thinking at the moment!"

I'd grown to distrust my weather app because it had been consistently underestimating wind speeds. Right now, it was predicting 12–20-mile-an-hour wind pretty much all day, but I didn't tell VO that.

I didn't sleep well last night. Loud banging noises from the coal energy plant across the river continued on and off throughout the night. Such were the annoyances of urban paddling.

As the wind ramped up overnight, small waves lapped against the shore. Camping along a river with locks and dams always makes me alert for a sudden rise in water level, because we never know when a lockmaster might choose to let out more water for some reason. A rapid water level rise of a couple of feet wasn't unheard of on this river.

When I finally crawled out of my tent in the dark at 7:15 a.m., the river was only about five feet from my tent and within a foot or two of our boats. We were camped on a rocky spot that was only a foot above the water line.

We'd planned for this scenario last night. "If the river rises up to our tents," I'd said to VO when we decided to camp here, "we should figure out the quickest way to get to higher ground." I pointed to a nearby rise.

The fire last night was fantastic. There was plenty of dry driftwood all over the shoreline. Nothing like camping along a river with a nice campfire to sit by. And a little bourbon to take the edge off.

But back to the wind ...

I got ready faster this morning, anticipating high winds in the afternoon, and I was packed up and on the water by 8:15. VO hadn't even taken his tent down yet, but I knew he'd be able to catch up to me in no time if I headed out before him.

The wind was steady out of the southeast right from the start. Another perfect morning except for the wind. At first it was blowing a steady five to seven miles an hour. Having an overactive mind when the paddling was hard just made the situation worse for me, so I focused on a Zen state, like Seth suggested, and quietly sang paddling songs to myself. I settled into a pace I felt I could sustain throughout the day given the wind. That calmed me down.

I stopped to chat with three guys who were working on their tied-off pontoon boat. We talked about the river and the wind and the lack of current while I rested my arms a bit. We all agreed that some of the tugs and tows on this river were so quiet they could sneak up behind you. One guy said he'd almost been run over twice in the past couple of years.

After another mile, I paddled past the small village of Bethlehem, where I stopped to talk with a guy who was doing some work on his dock. The wind was picking up, and I had to keep paddling just to stay in place while we talked. Bethlehem had some beautiful homes along the river, and his was one of them.

It was an hour and a half since I'd shoved off, and I only had three miles under my belt. Now, VO was pulling up behind me. He continued the conversation with the guy while I paddled off into what was not quite a ten-mile-an-hour headwind. We'd agreed before I started out this morning that we'd cross left to the Kentucky shoreline somewhere around Bethlehem. But the river continued to turn to the right, so the shortest route was to stay along the right bank.

I paddled on.

Around mile 4, I decided that it was now or never to cross over to the left, since the wind was getting stronger and the waves bigger. Whitecaps were forming in the middle of the river.

I told VO I would start across but said if the water got too choppy in the first hundred yards, I'd head back to the Indiana shoreline. The waves were big enough to have me right on the edge of my comfort zone, but I decided to keep paddling across.

At one point, a big pleasure boat zipped past a few hundred yards away, kicking up big waves. When its powerful wake combined with the existing waves and the wind, it seemed like waves were coming from every direction.

Deep breaths.

Exhale.

Keep paddling into the waves.

I was having trouble turning my bow into some of the bigger waves. My left rudder pedal felt jammed, and I had to paddle harder on one side or the other to get my boat to turn into the waves.

About eighty percent of the way across, I looked behind me and realized I'd never dropped my rudder into the water. No wonder my rudder pedal wasn't working! I laughed out loud at myself.

The wind kept picking up. For the next four to five miles, it blew over twenty miles an hour. And the waves continued to build.

We were paddling about one mile an hour. Slow. To stop paddling, even for a moment, meant drifting backward. It finally got to the point where despite paddling hard, we couldn't move forward at all. The waves were too big. We hugged the shoreline, but the shallow water just made the waves swell even higher.

Despite this, I was in a good headspace. Paddling with a strong, consistent rhythm and inching along. Literally. *If we make it fifteen miles today*, I thought, *we'll be lucky*.

Then the wind cranked itself up to the next level.

I had to paddle as hard as I could just to stay in one place and keep my bow into the waves. I wasn't moving at all. It was the kind of wind that would be hard even to walk in. We pushed on another half mile or so, moving no faster than half a mile an hour. It was noon and we'd only gone nine miles, but now we'd slowed almost to a complete halt.

I had to put all my paddling energy into just staying upright and keeping waves from splashing over the sides of my canoe. We were only ten yards from shore, so it wasn't dangerous, just insanely slow and exhausting. Still, tipping over in my fully loaded boat would be a major fiasco.

VO finally yelled over the wind, "Let's pull off the first place we can!" In a hundred yards or so I saw a small, sandy spot in front of a house, just on the edge of the town of Westport, Kentucky.

We paddled hard into the shore and pulled our boats out of the water as fast as we could so the waves wouldn't bash them against the bank. Even that was grueling.

We both flopped down on the ground, exhausted. What now?

There was no use paddling in this wind, and it was only getting worse.

Google Maps showed the Westport marina only a quarter mile farther downriver. We debated whether we'd be able to get our loaded boats back into the water, let alone climb into them, with these gigantic waves.

We decided to give it a try and head for the marina, because where we'd pulled our boats out wasn't anywhere near a road. VO's wife, Val, was planning to meet us at the end of the day in Louisville, Kentucky, but if we could at least get to the marina in Westport, she could meet us there instead.

Paddling that last quarter mile was crazy. I'd plow five to ten paddle strokes into the three-foot waves, then use the next few strokes to align my bow in the right direction while the waves pushed me backward toward the shore. I'd regroup, get my bow reoriented, then push ahead a few more feet.

I was ecstatic when the boat ramp finally came into view. That was at 12:30 p.m., four and a half hours after we'd started out this morning. We'd only gone nine and a half miles, but this would have to be it for the day.

Going any farther just wasn't an option, so we unloaded our boats at Schamback Park in Westport and called it a day. We hauled our boats up near a picnic table, stowed most of our gear underneath, then cable-locked the boats together.

It is 2:30 p.m. now, and we just had a fantastic lunch at a cafe called Knock On Wood a few blocks from the park.

The trees outside the cafe were still bending over in the wind. The high winds were supposed to continue through the rest of the day and into the evening. This was our second "weather day" of the trip, but at least we got nine and a half miles in. My paddling cousin Jeff always used to say, "You take what the river—and weather—gives you." But being mentally and psychologically okay with that can be tough sometimes.

DAY 28

October 14, 2024

Westport, KY, to Captain's Quarters marina

15½ miles
Total: 596 miles

Towns and locks: Sunset Village (584), Utica (596)

Wind, wind, and more wind.

Today was the third day in a row of high winds.

Saturday afternoon, all day Sunday, and now Monday. All nonstop wind.

We stopped yesterday after only 9½ miles, and today we only got in 15½. Combined, that equaled one full day of paddling lost.

We stayed in a nice hotel in downtown Louisville last night. And this morning we were back to the river in Westport by 9:00. We left most of our stuff in our rooms and paddled with empty boats today since Val was hanging around and we'd be returning to our hotel again tonight.

Once again, our weather apps underestimated the winds. We knew the second we hit the water that the wind and waves were almost as bad as when we had started out yesterday. Whitecaps covered the river. Enormous, back-to-back waves. At least enormous when you're sitting in a small boat. Wind at fifteen miles an hour and gusting to twenty-five. The gusts not only produced big waves, but millions of mini-waves along the surface of the water.

Pushing the blade of the out-of-water end of my kayak paddle met with almost as much wind resistance as the opposite blade that was digging into the water. To stop paddling to scratch my nose or adjust my sunglasses meant blowing backward.

I was in a good frame of mind today, knowing we'd only paddle as far as we could, and it would all be okay. And we had a nice hotel room and a hot shower to return to tonight.

It started out chilly at only forty-five degrees, and it never got above fifty-six all day. I was cold all day long. I wore short pants, like I always do, no matter the temperature, and had a windbreaker over my long-sleeved polypro shirt. And just my Packers cap on my bald head. I hadn't put on enough warm clothes today, and everything else was in my hotel room. I wouldn't make that mistake tomorrow.

After two hard hours of paddling, we pulled off into a tiny, stagnant creek to rest our arm muscles and pee. As I climbed out of my canoe, my right foot plunged into the mud right up to my calf. I *could not* pull my foot out without leaving my water sandal behind in the deep muck. It took me several minutes, bracing myself against my boat with my left knee in the water, to eventually extract my muddy leg and foot out of the muck with my sandal still attached. I actually felt a little panicky for a minute, recalling the quicksand I'd gotten stuck in on the Mississippi River several years ago.

After the first four and a half miles, the river turned southwest, and the wind was coming out of the northwest. We still had an incessant wind in our faces, but it wasn't as bad, and we could finally paddle about three miles an hour. As the wind continued to shift toward the south, we got a small combination of tailwind and crosswind—our first tailwind in the last several days.

Around mile 9½, we stopped at a marina to eat the peanut butter and jelly sandwiches we'd made this morning in the hotel's breakfast room. We tied off our boats to a finger of a dock and climbed out. I was soaked after my incident in the mud, and it was still windy. I immediately started shivering, so I stuffed down my sandwich, got back into my boat, and started paddling again just to warm up. My wet feet were frozen, my hands were stiff, and I could tell I was getting hypothermic.

We paddled 6 more miles and stopped at 3 p.m. after putting in 15½ miles for the day. A good effort in this wind. Over the past two days we'd only paddled 26 miles, which added more time to our trip, but it was unavoidable.

Dinner at Burgers, Brews, and Bourbon in Louisville. The name said it all.

DAY 29

October 15, 2024

Captain's Quarters marina to Riverview Park boat ramp, mile 619

23 miles
Total: 619 miles

Towns and locks: Louisville (603), McAlpine Lock and Dam (606½), New Albany (608½)

Chilly and breezy as we pulled onto the river this morning. Overcast. Mild headwind.

As we neared downtown Louisville, about five miles into our paddle, a headwind picked up and the water got choppy and squirrely. Wind, waves, and boat traffic: the trifecta that made big-river paddling a challenge—and a little unnerving.

Once we made it through the McAlpine Lock and Dam, the river turned south and we got a tailwind for the first time in several days. But dark, black clouds loomed to the north over Indiana, and I was hoping they would move off.

We paddled on.

Around 2 p.m., it started raining big, cold, hard drops, then hailed for about ten minutes. I guess those clouds weren't moving off to the north after all. I was on my daily paddling phone call with my mom, and I had to hang up to focus on the rain and hail.

By the time I dug to the bottom of my day pack to get my raincoat, I was soaked and getting chilled, so I just threw my raincoat over my life jacket. I spread my plastic map case over my soaked pants to help keep some heat in. It only rained for fifteen minutes, but it was too late. I would be wet and cold for the rest of the day.

I had dressed a little differently today. I wore long pants for the first time in the last twenty-nine days, my fleece hat, a heavy fleece sweatshirt over my t-shirt, and a windbreaker over all that for most of the day. I also wore my neoprene paddle boots for the first time on the trip.

I'll need to wear even more tomorrow since the day will start out ten degrees colder, just above freezing. We're into the second half of October now, and temperatures are dropping.

We paddled past dozens of mansions, mostly on the Kentucky side, perched high above the built-up riverbank. Gigantic. As we neared Louisville, we passed a water treatment plant that had a sign showing the high-water mark of the Ohio River in 1937—high water that had flooded sixty percent of Louisville. The mark was at least thirty-five feet above my head. It was hard to imagine what this massive river would be like if it were thirty-five feet higher!

After paddling under four bridges, past the KFC Yum! Center where I had seen the Dalai Lama several years ago, and past the historic Galt House Hotel, we entered a man-made channel that led to two large lock chambers.

This channel had been built to bypass a steep drop and waterfall on the main river. We called the lockmaster and thankfully, we were able to paddle right up to the "land side" lock. The massive gates opened, a loud horn blew, the stop-and-go light—like those mounted on the entry of every Army Corps lock—changed from flashing red to flashing green, and we paddled into the chamber.

Val picked us up at Riverview Park in Greenwood, Kentucky, at mile 23 for the day. We stashed our boats in some riverside weeds, cable-locked them together, and took off for the New Albanian Brewery in New Albany, Indiana, a favorite beer-drinking spot for Leslie and me when we lived in Bloomington, Indiana.

It was nice to get some decent miles in after a couple of windy, low-mileage days.

DAY 30

October 16, 2024

Riverview Park boat ramp to Tobacco Landing near Laconia, IN

22½ miles
Total: 641½ miles

Towns and locks: West Point (630½)

I always think of things to write about when I'm paddling. But when it comes time to journal, my mind usually goes blank. Maybe it's because I'm exhausted by the end of each day.

We are camped at a spot on the river called Tobacco Landing, near a small, dried-up creek. We'd pulled off to check around for a camping spot, and up above the river a ways was a small gravel parking area. Now, we are all set up and have a nice fire going. I bought some cheese, crackers, and pickles yesterday in Louisville, so we enjoyed hors d'oeuvres and a few shots of an excellent rye whiskey VO bought called Angel's Envy.

Evenings like this make the hard days worth all the work—almost.

It was hard to leave our comfy hotel in Louisville after spending the last three nights there. I walked down the street again this morning to get some good coffee before heading out. Val drove us back to Riverview Park by 8:30, and we were on the water by 9.

It was a chilly forty-six degrees when we started paddling. I started out with two heavy long-sleeved shirts and a windbreaker, long underwear bottoms beneath my long pants, warm hat and gloves, and heavy socks inside my neoprene booties.

I noticed when I was paddling that my paddle seemed heavier, which was weird. My arms felt like they were lifting more weight with every stroke. You'd think that after paddling for thirty days, my arms would be getting stronger. Maybe it was just the extra layers of clothes I was wearing.

The riverbanks today were surprisingly rural given how close we still were to the big city of Louisville. Just trees, trees, and more trees. Beautiful, peaceful scenery.

For the first three hours, we had a bit of a tailwind, and the paddling was actually fun. We zipped along at about four miles an hour, and by noon had gone 13 miles. I began to entertain the thought of a 28–30-mile day.

But around noon, the river turned from south to due west, and we got hit by the wind that had been pushing us along all morning. Then the river turned northwest and we got slammed.

"This wind is worse than the day we only went nine and a half miles!" VO yelled. The waves weren't as bad, but the wind was fierce. Long, hard pulls on my kayak paddle only generated about half a mile an hour of speed. And we did that for the next three hours.

We wanted to be on the Kentucky side of the river, on the left, but the wind and waves were too big for me to cross over. Too many whitecaps. I knew I'd regret it once I got out in the middle of the river. At one point, I paddled maybe a hundred yards toward the middle of the river, then got scared and raced back as fast as I could to the Indiana shoreline.

"We aren't getting anywhere!" I finally shouted back to VO at 3 p.m. "We could cover this distance tomorrow morning in minutes!" By 3:45, we had decided to head for Tobacco Landing, a spot that showed up on both our Ohio River Guide map and Google Maps.

We could have easily paddled for another hour or more, but we were barely moving and were both ready to be done. So we called it. Twenty-two and a half miles would have to be good enough.

At 6 p.m., it was getting cold again. It was supposed to get down to thirty-four degrees tonight, so we were in for a cold morning, no doubt with frost on our tents and boats.

Two nights ago, I had a really vivid dream. It stuck with me all the next day, so I described it to Val, who is a therapist, hoping for her interpretation.

I was crossing a snow bridge that spanned a crevasse on a big, snowy mountain, trying to get to a lodge where I had two friends waiting. I was on a climbing trip but traveling alone. When I approached the snow bridge, it seemed to be shifting a bit. The snow was moving slightly. So I raced across quickly, and just when I got to the other side, the snow bridge collapsed and slid down the mountain, triggering a massive avalanche.

The avalanche I'd started triggered an even bigger one above me that swept over the lodge I was heading toward. I was in a safe spot, but I stood there and watched several people I knew, including my two friends, get swept down the mountain.

I knew everyone was buried in the snow and ice. I also knew they were all dead. I continued up to the lodge. It was still standing, and there were people there, milling around in a state of shock. I talked with them about wanting to be part of the search and recovery efforts.

It was already dark, and I was told there wouldn't be any efforts to look for survivors until morning. I knew the cold would likely kill anyone who had survived the avalanche. People said there would be a helicopter search for survivors in the morning that I could join.

In the moment, I had a sudden strong need to go to my parents' house to make sure they knew I was okay. It was like a compulsion. I had to get home. So I hitchhiked all night, in the pitch dark, to get there. Then I woke up.

"Any interpretations?" I asked Val.

"A dream starting with a bridge is very meaningful," she said. "It could represent going from a place of danger to a place of safety."

Throughout the dream, despite the dangers, I was never afraid. I felt very confident and in control of myself. I was worried about others and very sad for the tragedy that had killed my friends, but I was not worried about myself or my safety.

Val said my need to get "home" was significant. Not necessarily to my parents' house, but just the idea of home itself, and needing to get there as soon as possible.

She asked if the friends who had died were people I knew in real life, but I couldn't name anyone specifically.

Averting tragedy. Watching a tragedy unfold. I wondered, as I told Val about the dream, whether I'd caused the avalanche and the deaths. But it didn't feel that way in the dream. It seemed to me the avalanche happened on its own, as the snow had already been shifting around when I got to the snow bridge. I was just lucky enough to notice it and avoid it. And powerless to do anything about it.

So ...

DAY 31

October 17, 2024

Tobacco Landing to Leavenworth, IN (The Dock)

22½ miles
Total: 664 miles

Towns and locks: Brandenburg (646), Mauckport (648), Leavenworth (654)

We're at a restaurant called The Dock in Leavenworth, Indiana, sitting at a picnic table and charging our devices, journaling, and meeting locals. So happy to be here!

A bucket of Corona. Dinner ordered.

We just talked with Scott, a super nice local guy. He said he and his wife, Marianne, and his girls, Olive and Chloe, came here several times a week. Scott was very interested in our trip. Asked lots of questions. At one point, I told Kent, the owner of the restaurant, and Scott that I would write about them in my Ohio River book.

"Make sure to mention Marianne, Olive, and Chloe in your book, too!" Marianne yelled from several tables down.

Our waitress, Lilly, took our order. She looked all of sixteen years old but served our bucket of beers like a pro, so she made it into the book, too.

And then there was Kent, the owner of The Dock. He turned out to be the *man*!

We'd been planning to stop in Leavenworth tonight, so we had our eyes on this spot on the map all day long.

Earlier, we had paddled past the cute little town of Leavenworth to an RV campground on the outskirts. In this second half of October, it looked like almost all the campers were closed up for the season. We pulled off to ask a guy who was driving a riding lawnmower if we could set up our tents along the shore for the night.

His name was John. "Well," he said, "it's Indiana law that you can't have tents in a campground if there's no public restroom."

"What?" I had never heard of such a law.

"It's Indiana law and the RV park owner's rule that there can't be any tent camping here."

"We're happy to pay," I said. "And we don't need a washroom. We'll be gone first thing in the morning. We've been camping along the river for the past four weeks and we're pretty sure we haven't been breaking any laws."

"I'm really sorry, guys. There's another campground about six miles back upriver."

"But we're heading *that* way." I pointed downriver. "So I don't think we'll be paddling six miles back *up* the river."

"Well, sorry, guys. Good luck."

"Okay." I faked a smile. When John turned around to climb back onto his mower, I gave him my middle finger.

I asked VO to call The Dock to see if we could camp somewhere near their restaurant. Leavenworth, at least the older part of town along the river, only had a few houses and buildings, along with several mobile homes. Apparently, the massive flood of 2018 had wiped out the entire town. In the ensuing years, property sold for cheap, and very few people built permanent homes. They just brought in trailers.

Kent, who had bought The Dock last year after it had been closed for five years post-flood, answered the phone.

"Hi," I said. "My buddy and I are paddling the Ohio River, and today is Day 31. We want to come over to The Dock and get dinner and drink beer, but we were hoping you also had a spot where we could set up our tents for the night."

"Absolutely. Canoe on over."

We had to paddle back upriver about a quarter mile, but it was so worth it. Kent met us outside the restaurant and pointed out several grassy spots across the street where we could set up our tents. He was the nicest guy. Totally into the fact that we were taking a break from our adventure to stop and eat at his restaurant.

He listened to some of our stories as we drank his cold beer, and asked if he could take a picture with us outside next to a gigantic wooden deck chair. I told Kent we'd let the Ohio River Trail folks know about how welcoming and friendly he was.

The Dock had live music every Thursday, Friday, Saturday, and Sunday night. All year long! As luck would have it, today was Thursday.

The menu was simple but good. I ordered a mahi-mahi sandwich, and VO had the pulled pork tenderloin. We shared a bucket of Corona with lime slices.

Kent stopped by our table a couple of times to make sure we were doing okay. He just seemed thrilled that a couple of small-time "celebrities" had stopped in. What a find—a great place to stop, eat, drink, and camp. So happy that knucklehead at the RV park wouldn't let us camp there.

Today's paddling was fantastic! That might be my third Corona talking, but still.

Seven hours of paddling is long and tedious no matter what the conditions, but the weather could not have been better. It got down to thirty-four degrees last night, but I was cozy warm in my sleeping bag and lightweight down blanket. I actually slept better than most previous nights.

I decided to support VO's sleeping in until 7:30 a.m. He'd been nervous about the cold temps last night and tonight, but today he said, "It wasn't as bad as I thought." VO is a Florida boy, and cold for him is low sixties.

I put on long underwear and long pants this morning and wore my down jacket and warm hat during breakfast. My hot oatmeal and instant Starbucks tasted especially good this chilly morning.

Despite not crawling out of my tent until 7:30, I was still on the water by 9, with VO following shortly after.

It was a perfect paddling day. No wind. Almost totally flat water. Cloudless. This stretch of the Ohio River was mostly untouched. Almost no houses. No industry. Just trees on the verge of turning their fall colors and some rocky bluffs on the Indiana shoreline.

I saw several groups of deer drinking water on the river's edge. A couple of bald eagles kept their eyes on us. And I saw the head of a small river otter or mink poke up above the water, then dive back down as I paddled closer.

Just a perfect day for a paddle. A long, perfect day. I could almost convince myself I was just out for a day paddle and not on Day 31 of a thousand-mile river trip.

I'll remember Kent's hospitality as much as Scott and his family's curiosity about our trip.

If we can keep paddling twenty-two or twenty-three miles a day, we'll only have 14 days left. Hard to believe. That's still a lot of days, but we have 31 in our rearview mirror already.

DAY 32

October 18, 2024

Leavenworth, IN, to Flint Island, KY

25 miles
Total: 689 miles

Towns and locks: Alton (679), Magnet (683)

Last night at The Dock, we each indulged in a cup of ice cream. I got butter pecan with hot fudge on top.

Fantastic.

As we packed up to leave this morning, I was thinking about another Kent we had met last night. As we were eating, I overheard parts of a conversation at Other Kent's table. They were talking about Kamala Harris going on Fox News yesterday for an interview—a very ballsy thing for her to do in my estimation.

I heard Other Kent and his group saying Kamala had dodged every question and gotten aggressive with the interviewer, Bret Baier. "Aggressive" is how I often hear older, conservative white men describe assertive women who speak up for themselves. Hillary Clinton had been similarly labeled. Anyway, it was clear who they were supporting for the 2024 presidential election, and it wasn't Kamala.

Just as we were getting ready to hunker down in our cold tents for the night across the street from The Dock, Other Kent and his wife came over to our table and offered to take us to their house for hot showers and asked if they could get anything for us from a nearby store. His wife even offered to bring us heaters for our tents. I'm not exactly sure how that would've worked, but it was a really nice offer on a cold evening. She couldn't get over the fact that we were camping tonight, when it was supposed to get below freezing.

We declined, but if she'd offered to let us sleep at their house in addition to taking a hot shower, I would've ditched our tents in a second.

Every night, whether it's warm or cold, I have the same routine. When I set up my tent, I put down a nylon ground cloth, blow up my Therm-a-Rest sleeping pad, then lay out my sleeping bag, small pillow, and down blanket. I set out my book, reading glasses, and headlamp. I also lay out a pair of boxers and a clean, dry t-shirt that I change into before bed. Tomorrow's clothes and my jacket for the morning go under my small pillow. I keep a water bottle for drinking and a Nalgene pee bottle within arm's reach. I also set out a bottle of Advil in case my achy muscles are keeping me awake.

Outside my rear tent door, beneath the vestibule, I keep bags of food and all my cooking stuff. That way, if it's raining in the morning, I have everything I need to cook in my vestibule. Inside my front door vestibule goes everything else, including my dry bags, cockpit bag, hat, sunglasses, and an extra water bottle. I don't like leaving things lying around outside.

Everything has its place, which makes everything easy to find in the middle of the night.

Today was another perfect-weather day. It was just thirty-four degrees when we got up, and there was the slightest bit of frost on our tents. It was hard crawling out of my toasty sleeping bag and into my frigid clothes.

But by 8:50, the sun was already warming things up, and VO and I were on the water. We paddled past the very small towns—if you could call them that—of Alton and Magnet, Indiana, heading for a boat ramp and small cluster of houses called Concordia, Kentucky.

The river really twisted and turned today. There were at least eight big bends, including one called Oxbow Bend.

Beautiful scenery: trees and small, rocky cliffs. Very rural. Again, it surprised me how rural this part of the Ohio River was. I just never knew.

Relaxing paddling. Calm winds. Cloudless sky.

We picked up a headwind at one point in the midafternoon, but after one more 180-degree turn in the river, it became a tailwind.

VO saw a beaver swimming. But other than that, just rhythmic, meditative paddling.

I had a good rock radio station on for part of the day. I also found a Louisville NPR station and listened to an interview with the producer of the series *Reservation Dogs*, a comedic series about reservation life from the perspective of five Native teens. It sounded awesome. I'd definitely watch it when I got home.

Being able to pick up stations that played more than just Christian or country and western music helped me better enjoy the seven or eight hours of paddling every day.

We'd planned to stop after 23 miles at the boat ramp in Concordia, but it was only 3:15 p.m. and the weather was perfect, so we paddled on 2 more miles to Flint Island, Kentucky.

There weren't any obvious spots to set up our tents, so we stopped on a sandy shoreline and hauled our stuff up a small, steep, sandy hill to a flat field of tall weeds on the outskirts of an unharvested soybean field. Not a great site, but good enough. We had to stomp down the head-high weeds to make room for our tents. It felt a little claustrophobic camping among tall weeds, but at least we were hidden from any farmers who might want to kick us out.

We even had a bit of a river view. I fried up some kielbasa with pinto beans, rice, and hot sauce. It was a great meal. I cooked the shit out of the meat, since I'd been carrying it around for three or four days since Louisville. It turned out fine. No bellyaches.

I can't help but count down the days. I'm trying to stay focused on appreciating where I am and enjoying the moments. I also can't think too much about being done, since we still have at least thirteen days to go. Today is Friday. Two weeks from today, I hope to be in a rental car on my way home to Pittsburgh and Leslie.

Coal barges passed by as we ate our dinner. One full coal barge going in each direction. Now what sense does that make? Bringing coal upriver and passing a coal barge coming from the direction you're heading.

Tomorrow, we plan to paddle to Cloverport, Kentucky, a small river town with a boat ramp and at least one restaurant. It even has a bourbon distillery that's open until 9 p.m. on Saturdays. That's a must-visit!

DAY 33

October 19, 2024

Flint Island, KY, to Cloverport, KY

22 miles
Total: 711 miles

Towns and locks: Derby (692½), Rome (701), Cloverport (711)

We're sitting in Smith Holler Distillery, our first distillery on the Ohio River.

Smith Holler is about half a mile outside of Cloverport, Kentucky. Well worth the short walk. The owner and distiller, Mike Smith, makes whiskey, vodka, and moonshine. He opened in February 2022, just two years ago. It's a must-stop if you're anywhere near Cloverport.

Mike served us a "taster" of his three distilled beverages and five flavored whiskey shots, all of which were amazing. One of the mixed shots was pink, and Mike crafted it in honor of Penny, a woman in Cloverport who had breast cancer. So we drank a shot for Penny.

I followed my whiskey flight with an old fashioned. After a few sips, I turned to VO and said, "We'd better get to journaling before we drink much more."

We had paddled up to the boat ramp in Cloverport around 4 p.m. There was a nice grassy area and covered picnic spot right along the river. I called the local police station and the city hall offices to see if we could camp at the boat ramp park. No one answered. I even tried the police twice, but no answer.

While I sat with our stuff, VO walked down Main Street a ways and saw some people setting up for "Music on Main," a community shindig that was going on this evening. Booths and tables were being set up along the sidewalk on both sides of the street. VO met Christine, who was setting up a table. She called the mayor, Candy, to ask about camping, and Candy said it was no problem.

We set up our tents on a nicely mown patch of grass. Our tents had been soaking wet this morning when we packed up, and my sleeping bag was damp, too, when I crammed it into my stuff sack. So it was nice to get our wet tents set up and aired out and put our sleeping bags out in the sun for a bit.

Once we were all set up, we headed down Main Street toward Smith Holler Distillery. On the way, we ducked into a little bar called Slow Time to see their menu and plan for dinner on our way back from Smith Holler.

We also poked our heads into Mayor Candy's Mile Marker 711, a little bar that sold lots of good bourbon. There were seven or eight people inside drinking cold Bud Lights, including three ladies who were looking at us like they knew us—or thought they did.

One of the women lit up. "You're the two paddlers we saw on The Dock's Facebook page!"

What?

Apparently, Kent had posted our picture on his Facebook page, and these ladies had seen it.

They encouraged us to check out the distillery. "Once you get there and start drinking," one of them said, "you may never leave." Another chimed in: "Tell them the ladies from Indiana said hello." It turned out they'd driven here from Indiana for the day and for Music on Main.

We told the ladies from Indiana we'd stop back at Candy's for a beer after our distillery visit, then we headed up the road and out of town to continue our quest to the distillery.

(VO and I are each on our second old fashioned after downing the flight of shots. VO seems especially talkative, and I'm especially buzzed. My journal handwriting is also starting to get illegible.)

It's 5:36 p.m. Central Time. We realized yesterday afternoon that we'd passed into the Central Time Zone. I had to watch a YouTube video a few minutes ago to figure out how to change the time on my Suunto watch. That means it will be getting dark by 6:30 p.m., and the sun will be rising around 7 a.m. now. That will help us get going at a decent time in the morning. We'll just need to be camped, set up, and eating dinner by 6 p.m. from here on out so we're not doing things in the dark.

Oh shit, I never even wrote about the paddling today. See? The old fashioneds are kicking in. It was super foggy this morning. Really dense. It was the thickest fog we'd paddled in so far on this trip. And it didn't burn off until 11. Everything was soaking wet when we packed up. I hate packing up wet stuff.

I was on the water by 8:50 a.m. and paddled for almost two hours before VO caught up and the fog started to burn off. He had given me his blessing to start out on my own. I know he doesn't like the pressure of me standing around, antsy to get going.

It's eerie to paddle in dense fog on a big river, knowing that tugboats and massive barges could be just a few feet away and out of sight. I always stay close enough to the shoreline that I can keep the riverbank in sight. It's too easy to get turned around or run over when you can only see ten to fifteen feet in any direction.

Once the fog had burned off, the banks displayed more beautiful trees. No houses for miles-long stretches. The water was flat calm until noon and then we picked up a five- or six-mile-an-hour headwind for the rest of the day.

When Cloverport came into view, I was happy to be done. VO wanted to go farther, but I was like ... a restaurant, a boat ramp, a grassy spot to camp, *and* a distillery? It was all too good to pass up. Paddle two or three more miles to ... what, exactly? We're stopping. And we were both glad we did.

DAY 34

October 20, 2024

Cloverport, KY, to Troy, IN

20 miles
Total: 731 miles

Towns and locks: Cannelton Lock and Dam (721), Hawesville (724), Tell City (727½), Troy (731)

The Music on Main festival last night was probably as big as things got in Cloverport. Three or four blocks of Main Street were blocked off. There were a handful of booths selling arts and crafts. There was one guy with a huge, welded metal bull that was actually a meat smoker, with smoke coming out of the bull's nostrils. A bluegrass band played live music.

It seemed like there were only a few dozen people milling around. But then again, there were probably only a couple of hundred residents in Cloverport to begin with.

Not only did the Indiana ladies at Candy's Mile Marker 711 recognize us from Facebook, but after drinking at the distillery, we stopped into Slow Time Bar for dinner, and the owners behind the bar recognized VO when he went up to pay. "Hey, aren't you the guys paddling the river?" one of them said.

Word gets around in these parts.

We had terrific smoked-brisket sandwiches from the smoky-nosed bull barbecue and washed them down with some weak, small-town bar beer.

We were in our tents by 8:30 p.m.

It was a cold night. My sleeping bag felt clammy.

The bluegrass music continued until 11:30 p.m. I knew that because it was keeping me awake. From the sound of it, the party had gotten a little rowdy toward the end of the night.

I was super thirsty all through the night with all that whiskey on board. And I peed a lot more than usual in the Nalgene bottle that I always keep next to me in the tent, next to a full water bottle in case I get thirsty. Usually, my water bottle is full, and my pee bottle is fairly empty, so I never confuse them in the dark of night. I can differentiate them by their weights. But last night I drank and peed a lot, so a couple of times I had to turn on my headlamp to make sure I knew which Nalgene bottle was which. At one point, I grabbed the fuller bottle, unscrewed the lid in the dark and brought it to my lips for a sip, and was hit with the rank smell of rancid pee.

Close call.

It was chilly getting out of the tent this morning. Given the change to Central Time, and the fact that the sun was now rising at 7 a.m. and not 8, I decided I was going to start rolling out of bed at 6:30 instead of 7:30.

Cold.

Humid.

Light fog over the water.

Down jacket.

Long pants.

Time to paddle.

The leaves were starting to turn. Lots more beautiful scenery. Rural paddling.

No wind.

Perfect paddling conditions.

I started out and paddled for about ninety minutes while VO finished packing his boat and hustled to catch up. I love this time of day. Cool temps. Quiet. Contemplative.

We paddled into the Cannelton lock around 10 a.m. I called the lockmaster about half a mile out like I always do. Initially, he said he'd be using the small chamber to lock a barge through ahead of us, so we'd have to wait. But then he said, "Oh, heck. Just keep on paddling and I'll lock you through first."

Awesome. We paddled up to the massive steel doors of the lock and he let us right in.

"Hey! Hello!"

I looked up to see a visitor standing on a viewing platform.

"Where are you paddling from?" he yelled down to us.

I stopped paddling. "Pittsburgh!"

His eyes widened. "What? Pittsburgh?"

"Yup, Pittsburgh!"

"That's amazing! Are you kidding?"

"No! Today is Day 34!" I started paddling again.

"Amazing!"

It's funny how little interactions like that, with disbelieving strangers, can be a real morale boost.

In the afternoon, I made a couple of lengthy work calls to pass the time.

We paddled ten more miles, past Tell City and on to Troy, Indiana, to meet up with my brother-in-law Keith and his partner, Anna. I'd been looking forward to this meetup for weeks. Long before we started this trip, I'd been hoping Keith and Anna would meet us somewhere along the river. After we stashed our boats, we piled into Keith and Anna's car and hung out at a fun restaurant for a few hours, just catching up and enjoying our conversation. It was so nice to spend a few hours with family.

DAY 35

October 21, 2024

Troy, IN, to Owensboro, KY

26 miles
Total: 757 miles

Towns and locks: Grandview (742), Rockport (748), Owensboro (757)

I'm exhausted.

But I'd rather be exhausted after paddling 26 miles than after only 18 or 20. Twenty-six miles feels good—a real accomplishment on this current-less river.

At 6:30 a.m. I called the one taxi company in Tell City, Indiana, which was where Keith and Anna had driven us to spend the night. I was a little nervous because I'd tried calling the taxi company several times last night to schedule a pickup for this morning, but no one answered. The Holiday Inn we were staying at was several miles from where we left our boats.

This morning, someone answered and agreed to meet us at the Holiday Inn at 7:45.

First, I want to go back to something that happened a few days ago, on Saturday ...

We had camped on this low spot on the river and had a great campfire that evening. About an hour into the paddle the next morning, I saw five older guys clad in biking leathers walking out onto a dock. As I paddled up, I saw five dual-sport motorcycles parked and covered in mud. These old guys were on an off-road bike trip.

I slowed down to say good morning.

The guys were super fascinated by our river trip. They were on a multi-day ride, and we were on a multi-day paddling trip. So we shared a few moments of respect for each other's adventures. I admired these guys in their sixties and seventies out riding big, dual-sport bikes—bombing around on their cool BMWs, Kawasakis, and Hondas.

They seemed to appreciate what VO and I were doing: spending thirty-five days on the river, paddling for seven or eight hours a day, every day, and seeing the Ohio River in a way that most people will never see it.

And later that same day ...

We were on the right side of the river. There was a point on the left bank where the river turned left, so we decided to cross over to shorten the paddling distance. VO always wanted to cut corners and paddle the shortest straight line between two points, even if that meant paddling in the middle of the river for forty-five minutes or a couple of miles. I'm more of the mind to get across the river to the opposite shore as quickly as possible and not hang out in the middle for any longer than necessary. I don't like loitering in the active shipping lane of the tugs and barges, so I usually cut straight across.

This time, for some reason, I took a look at that far point and decided to follow VO's strategy of paddling a long, straight line, taking a long path through the middle of the river. I turned and looked over my left shoulder to make sure there were no barges coming up behind us, then took off toward the middle.

There was no one there. Nothing coming.

VO was somewhere behind me. We'd just stopped for a stretch and pee break, and it usually took VO a little longer to climb back into his kayak cockpit and get situated. So I was a ways ahead. I paddled into the middle of the river—for maybe ten minutes—while I listened to some FM radio station.

At one point, I instinctually turned my head to the left to look back over my shoulder and saw a barge behind me and only fifty yards off to my left. Paddling on a big river with a tugboat pushing massive barges at ten miles an hour just fifty yards away from a tiny canoe that the captain likely can't even see is, in a word, terrifying.

I was way, way, *way* too close—and momentarily shocked that I hadn't heard a thing. I never heard the tug and those barges coming up behind me.

It scared me because I was paddling directly into the path of this oncoming barge. If I hadn't glanced back over my shoulder at that moment ...

I paddled as hard as I could back toward the right shoreline to get out of the way, fearing this massive barge would run right over me. In all my more than 150 days on the Mississippi, Tennessee, and Ohio Rivers, I had never been that close to getting run over by a barge.

Today's paddle went by quickly. It got up into the high seventies—this was late October—with not a cloud in the sky. I dumped at least half a dozen cups of cold river water over my head and down my back to cool off. This also woke me up a bit.

I made a couple of long work calls while I paddled, so that helped the time fly by. There was no wind until later in the day when we got a slight headwind. But it wasn't bad.

We'd originally planned to paddle to the start of Yellow Bank Island, a two-and-a-half-mile–long, super-skinny island that started at mile 23 for the day. We had planned to paddle a narrow channel that separated the island from the Indiana shoreline and look for campsites. But once we got to that spot, we both felt good, and even though it was already 4 p.m. and we'd been on the water for almost eight hours, we decided to paddle three more miles on to Owensboro, Kentucky, and find a hotel for the night.

Shower. Cozy bed. Good food. Plenty of motivation to keep paddling.

We paddled on to the English Park Boat Ramp, just past downtown Owensboro. We didn't pull up until after 5 p.m.

Nine hours on the water.

DAY 36

October 22, 2024

Owensboro, KY, to Newburgh, IN

21 miles
Total: 778 miles

Towns and locks: Newburgh Lock and Dam (776½), Newburgh (778)

Well. Today was a day I'd just as soon forget, for a few reasons:

1. Work-related frustrations kicking the day off
2. Scariest water yet
3. Newburgh not being very welcoming

I started my day off dealing with some very frustrating work emails. I'd been engaged with the U.S. Forest Service in negotiations regarding environmental monitoring for a silver mine expansion in Southeast Alaska. I thought we'd been working in good faith, and I'd put a lot of trust in the Forest Service to do the right thing. But emails this morning blew everything up and it put me in a foul mood.

Right from the start, I wasn't really into paddling this morning. I wasn't sure if it was the work thing or not. But I just couldn't get my head or my heart into it. For the first six or seven miles, I was just counting paddle strokes and marking off the morning in half-hour increments.

One hour down, six more to go ...

One and a half hours down, five and a half to go ...

You get the picture. Mental drudgery.

It was a bad way to paddle, glancing at my watch every few minutes.

But like I said, I was having a hard time getting into a good mental space and rhythm. Most days, I can clear my mind and the miles fly by. Not today.

At mile 3, we got to Little Hurricane Island and picked an inside channel close to the shore. The water was flat calm and there was no current. Lots of fall leaves floating on top of the water. We saw our bald eagle for the day. Seemed like we had seen at least one every morning. And a few blue herons.

Exiting the side channel and reentering the big river, the wind started to pick up. We decided to cross over to the Indiana shore so we could duck behind an upcoming set of islands that were two or three miles ahead.

By the time I got to the Indiana shore, the wind was blowing about ten miles an hour. It was a combination of a tailwind and crosswind, so it didn't really help. Instead, the wind just kept trying to push my boat up against the shore.

Taking waves broadside in a small canoe is not a good thing. I got a few splashes up on my lap. But I was even more agitated by the increasing wind and slow progress.

Around mile 7, I paddled past a boat ramp and a small marina, where I saw a sign for Coca-Cola. That looked like a great place to stop and take a break to regroup. But VO was way ahead of me, so I kept going, grumbling to myself as I paddled past the boat ramp.

After another three miles, I ducked behind an island and out of the wind for the most part. But the water felt thick and heavy, and I didn't seem to be moving very fast at all. Sometimes the water does that. It just feels heavy, like paddling through molasses.

As we neared the end of this fairly protected channel, I could see the Newburgh Lock and Dam way off in the distance.

I pointed at it. "That must be our next lock and dam," I said to VO. "It's still at least seven miles away, though."

VO raised his eyebrows. "Wow. That's actually very motivating."

"You know, it has the total opposite effect on me," I said, "when I can see something off in the distance but it's still seven miles away. Knowing it'll be another two and a half hours staring at something that doesn't seem to be getting any closer. I'd much rather have lots of little checkpoints to head to along the way."

The whole thing, including VO's optimism, just made me even more irritated.

As we paddled out from the island's protection, we were immediately pounded by a strong crosswind. I found out later it was blowing a consistent 15–20 miles an hour and gusting to 25. The waves were huge, and they rolled across the river from the opposite shore, building as they traveled and piling up as the water got shallower. Waves as high as one and a half feet slammed the side of my canoe every few seconds. A wave would grab my bow or stern at random and twist me around while another wave hit me broadside.

I stayed within thirty feet of the shore and kept getting pushed into shallower, rocky water. Waves crashed over my fabric spray deck and splashed into my cockpit and onto my lap. If I'd had more confidence, or been in a kayak, I would've paddled away from shore and into deeper water. The shallow water just compounds the size of the waves. But I was so worried about my canoe taking a big wave and rolling over that I stayed close to the shore.

It was very slow paddling.

It was very hard paddling.

It was very nerve-wracking.

And I started to get super frustrated with the situation.

I wasn't scared, though. Yet.

VO was way out in the middle of the river, paddling his straight line—the shortest distance between two points—while I hugged the shoreline. I thought he was crazy paddling out in the middle of the river, but kayaks can take waves over the bow with no problem.

I was getting pushed around all over the place. I slammed my left rudder pedal down, then my right pedal, to counter the waves that were alternately hitting my bow and stern and swinging me around. I had to maneuver constantly just to avoid tipping over.

VO must've sensed that I was in trouble, and he eventually paddled closer to shore. We stayed close to each other from then on.

With about three miles to go to the lock, we paddled past four industrial sites that each had several huge barges tied off and rafted together. To get around the barges, we had to paddle out away from the shore and toward the middle of the river. In choppy waters like these, the waves hit the sides of the barges, then bounced back in the opposite direction, forming clusters of waves that crashed from every direction.

Paddling farther away from shore made me nervous. Scared actually. I pulled the center spray skirt part of my fabric spray deck up over my lap in an attempt to keep some of the water out of my canoe.

The waves were getting bigger. The wind increased to a steady twenty-five miles an hour, still coming across the river from my left side. After a while, we pulled behind a tied-off barge to decide what to do.

"It's your call," VO said. "You're more exposed than I am. We can just stop here if it feels too unsafe."

I looked at the steep, slippery bank and dense trees and shrubs to my right, then out at the mounting waves to my left while bobbing around for a couple of minutes, temporarily out of the wind.

I decided to try paddling out into the mayhem again.

Almost immediately, I regretted my decision.

The water had turned crazy and chaotic. Waves were coming from every direction at once. Right side. Left side. Front. Back.

Crazy, confused, turbulent waters.

Once I was in it, I couldn't turn my boat around and go back. We paddled past a tugboat that was kicking out waves behind it. It was pushed up against a huge barge, keeping it in place. I couldn't tell for sure, but it looked like it was backing up into our path.

I knew we needed to paddle out farther toward the middle of the river to avoid the tug's backwash. The captain stepped out of the bridge and hollered that he'd wait for us to paddle around him.

Then the water got even worse.

We were a couple of hundred yards out from shore and had to paddle past several barges and another tug before I could head back closer to shore again. But the chaotic, crashing waves were so bad, and I came so close to capsizing several times, that I decided my only option was to paddle farther into the middle of the river.

Farther away from shore.

There was an island about half a mile away I thought I could tuck in behind to get out of the wind. If I could get to it.

Paddling out toward the middle of the river quickly became terrifying.

Even though it was sunny and bright, I had to keep my sunglasses off so I could read the water and waves and judge what was coming from which direction.

Every crashing wave made me hold my breath and get ready to be dumped into the river. About a quarter mile from shore, the chaos seemed to lessen. Even though the waves and wind stayed big, the waves were mostly coming from my left and behind me. The rebound waves from the barges and the waves piling up from the shallower water had lessened.

VO and I both made a turn back toward the right shore rather than continuing to the island and slowly inched back out of the middle of the river.

We had another mile of wind and waves to get to the lock, but the feeling of being in a blender was over.

Once inside the lock chamber, I immediately relaxed and felt a combination of exhilaration, residual fear, and gratefulness that I hadn't capsized in the middle of an active shipping lane.

On the other side of the lock, Newburgh was only a mile and a half away. It stayed windy, but it wasn't nearly as bad as it had been.

We were done for the day.

DAY 37

October 23, 2024

Newburgh, IN, to Henderson, KY

24 miles
Total: 802 miles

Towns and locks: Evansville (793)

Day 37 on the river! That's hard to believe. And we've paddled 36 of those 37 days with only the one day off for Hurricane Helene.

It's been a long trip.

It's getting harder and harder to psych up each morning to keep going. Of course I will, and we'll get to the Mississippi River, but it's getting harder.

We have 8 days left, weather willing.

Yesterday late afternoon, we paddled into the Newburgh boat ramp at the Old Lock and Dam Building No. 47. We pulled off after a long, hard, and scary day of paddling. We were beat.

The parking area adjacent to the boat ramp and grassy lawn was all out in the open, so I called the local police department to ask permission to camp at or near the boat ramp.

The police dispatcher relayed my request to an officer, who called me back a few minutes later.

The officer was courteous but immediately said camping was illegal in Newburgh. I told him our story. Thirty-six days on the river. Thru-paddling the entire Ohio River.

"Nope. No camping anywhere in the city limits, unfortunately."

"Do you know anyone who lives on or near the river who would let us set up our tents for the night?"

“I sure don’t. You could paddle on to Evansville, fifteen miles away, and see if you can camp there.”

I sighed. “It’s 4:30 p.m. We’re not going to paddle fifteen more miles tonight.”

“Well, I’m sorry. Maybe you could go across the river to the Kentucky side and camp there. That isn’t in our jurisdiction.”

“We were hoping to get a meal tonight, maybe breakfast in the morning. We’re visitors to your community. Tourists.”

“I’m sorry. I can’t help you.”

I hung up and immediately found the number for the City of Newburgh. I called and left a message for the city manager, Chris Cooke.

This had happened plenty of times before on long-distance thru-paddles. A couple of years ago, when I was on the Tennessee River, a state park ranger wouldn’t let us stay in the campground and suggested we paddle to another campground five miles back in the direction we had just come from.

Of the dozens and dozens of river towns I’ve paddled past on the Mississippi, Tennessee, and Ohio Rivers, there are some folks who recognize what we’re doing and the situation we’re in and will bend over backward to help us in some way. Then there are people like this Newburgh, Indiana, police officer who are following their rules and are unwilling to help. Life on the river.

We eventually stowed our canoes and camping gear off to the side of the ramp and caught an Uber to a local hotel. After we’d settled in, I got a call from Chris Cooke, the city manager. He was awesome. He apologized profusely for not being able to call me back sooner. He said he definitely could have worked something out to let us camp along the river.

Chris said he would contact the chief of police and explain that visitors who come to Newburgh by river are no different than visitors who come by car. “Newburgh is a river town,” he said, “and you are visitors to our community. We should’ve done better.”

I assured Chris I had no interest in getting the officer we’d talked to in trouble, and I encouraged him instead to make this a teachable moment and talk with his city council and police force about finding ways to be more accommodating to overnight river paddlers. Before he hung up, Chris asked me to connect him to the Ohio River Way organization so he could become part of that network and make his community more paddler friendly.

I really appreciated Chris's call.

On to today ...

We took off from the Newburgh boat ramp at 8:20 a.m. The river was flat calm, like glass. For the first mile.

Then the predicted wind started. First as a breeze, then a consistent wind. We were heading west, then northwest. Over the next three hours, the wind picked up and the waves grew. One- to one-and-a-half–foot waves with occasional whitecaps. And it seemed like no matter which way the river turned, the wind slammed us in the face. It was a long and slow paddle to Evansville, Indiana.

We had great views of the city from the river as we approached. In Evansville, the Ohio River makes a 180-degree turn back on itself. After an exhausting five hours of paddling, we turned south and finally had the strong winds at our back.

Same big waves. It's unnerving to paddle a small, loaded canoe with a fifteen-mile-an-hour tailwind and sizable waves piling up over your stern. You have to stay alert. But we sped right through the remaining nine miles to the boat ramp in Henderson, Kentucky.

Another long day.

The waves were so big today that it was even hard to get our boats unloaded and pulled out of the water. Our boats kept getting pushed around and smashed by waves coming ashore.

There wasn't anywhere to camp along the river near the boat ramp at Atkinson Park. And with the wind and waves, we were done paddling for the day. So, once again, I called the local police station to see if we could set up our tents in the park up above us.

Nope. It was illegal to camp anywhere in Henderson. What is with these river towns along the Ohio River?

The officer told me that earlier in the year, when the "no camping" ordinance was passed, the police had forced a family who had been living along the river for five years to move, as they were now violating the ordinance.

"Homeless people are not campers," I said. "They're survivors, not campers."

The officer wasn't interested in my ethical debate. He suggested we paddle back to Evansville, which was eight miles backward and into the wind. I again explained our situation and assured him we would stay out of the way and be gone by 8 a.m.

Nope.

Totally unhelpful. Totally unsupportive.

VO and I had been really looking forward to camping tonight. Oh well. The officer also told us we couldn't stow our boats in the trees for the night, but we did anyway. Out of sight. I had brought a long cable and lock on the trip, so on nights like tonight, we just cabled them together. In over 175 days on big rivers, I've never once had anyone mess with my boat or any gear stowed underneath.

DAY 38

October 24, 2024

Henderson, KY, to Winston Island

25 miles
Total: 827 miles

Towns and locks: Henderson (803)

We're all set up on tiny Winston Island, just a mile or two before the town of Mt. Vernon, Indiana. Winston Island is literally a stone's throw from the Indiana shoreline, yet my map says it's part of Kentucky.

We had a great paddling day. Got in twenty-five miles and finished by 3:45 p.m. We gathered a pile of driftwood and I got a fire started.

We are camped on a tiny sandy spot at the head of Winston Island, just a few feet from the water. Sitting in our collapsible camp chairs about four feet from the water's edge, we're sipping the whiskey I bought from the distillery in Cloverport. With the wind gone, the river is flat calm.

The bright embers of the fire warmed my bare legs.

Perfect.

I was thinking about seeing Leslie tomorrow.

I dug out the cheese and crackers and pickles I'd been carrying for several days. I threw the two pieces of cheese that had the most mold into the river, and VO and I ate the rest. I was in no mood to cook dinner, so cheese, crackers, pickles, and whiskey would have to be enough for tonight.

Paddling conditions today had been perfect. Twenty-five miles was still a long day of paddling. We had a very slight tailwind. Not enough for a big push, but still way better than a headwind.

We saw our daily morning eagle at 10 a.m. And I'm hearing one in the distance tonight as the sun goes down.

Tomorrow will bring what it brings. There is a chance of rain and thunderstorms with predicted winds out of the south at ten miles an hour. I'm not going to stress about it at the moment, though. Tomorrow will get here soon enough.

With seven days left on this adventure, my mind is drifting to work responsibilities, home projects, upcoming holiday plans, and the like. It's just part of allowing my mind to slowly reintegrate the rest of my life into my adventure paddling life.

Part of the reason I engage in long-distance adventures—canoeing, hiking, biking, climbing—is to escape those other responsibilities and mind clutter. But I always know that I have to return at some point. I want to return to that other world of my loves, my work, my neighbors, my house. I don't want to stay away forever.

I always return a little more appreciative, with my mind and my spirit a little less cluttered.

DAY 39

October 25, 2024

Winston Island to mile 847

20 miles
Total: 847 miles

Towns and locks: Mt. Vernon (829), Uniontown (842), John T. Myers Lock and Dam (846)

Leslie came to meet us. That was the highlight of the day. Of the week!

We had a tough time finding a place to pull off the river where Leslie could pick us up. No marinas, no towns, no boat ramps. No roads running alongside the river.

Our plan had been to pull off the river right after we paddled out of the John T. Myers lock chamber. Pull our boats up on the shore, grab our bags, and walk across federal property to the public parking lot to meet up with Leslie.

Well, I made the mistake of asking the lock employee, who was up above us when we paddled into the lock chamber, if there was a place we could pull out our boats at the end of the chute, just past the lock and dam. I made it very clear that we just wanted to walk to the public parking lot and that we would return in the morning.

The employee suggested we paddle back upriver three miles to Uniontown on the Kentucky side, which would add an hour and a half to Leslie's drive today—and our return to the river tomorrow morning. Not really an option.

"I need to ask the boss," the guy said several times.

"Great. Could you please ask him for us?"

The guy came back before he opened the massive lock doors to let us out. "The boss said no. You're not allowed to walk on the grass to the public parking lots. It's U.S. government property, and we don't want hunters and fishermen on the property."

"Well, we aren't either of those," I countered. "We're paddling the Ohio River and just need to meet my wife, who's meeting us this afternoon."

"The boss said no."

"What's your boss's name?"

"Bill Smith." (Not his real name.)

"I'll make sure to get some feedback to Bill's boss once this trip is over."

There was a *public* parking lot and a *public* viewing area at the lock. The *public* was obviously already allowed to walk from one to the other. But Bill wouldn't allow us to walk from the end of the lock chute to the lock parking lot?

While we were bobbing around in the lock chamber waiting for the water level to drop so we could paddle out the other side, a different lock employee poked his head over the edge of the lock wall to get my attention. *Shit,* I thought, *this is probably Bill. He must've heard me yell, "This is bullshit!" as we paddled into the lock chamber.*

But it wasn't Bill, it was another lock worker. "Bill's just being a dick," he said. "He's just an assistant here. The main lockmaster would have let you pull out and walk to meet your wife."

He glanced behind him, then continued: "If you wait until 4:30, Bill will be off work, and he won't be here tomorrow morning when you come back. Don't tell anyone I said this, but I think you should just paddle out of the lock chamber, hide your canoe in the weeds, and walk back through the woods. Just don't get caught."

When the massive lock doors opened, we paddled out and decided that since Bill had already said no, we shouldn't push getting caught. Violating some kind of federal law wasn't high on my list of things to get caught doing this afternoon.

We paddled about three-quarters of a mile past the lock and pulled off to find a road we'd seen on Google Maps. We climbed up a steep bank and pushed through some thick brush and swarms of mosquitoes but couldn't find any sign of a road. Since we couldn't have lugged our gear and boats up the steep bank anyway, we paddled farther and found a spot where a dirt road came closer to the river.

We dragged our canoes up onto a sandy shore, left most of our stuff with the boats, grabbed a couple of overnight bags, and walked about half a mile to a locked gate that connected to the dirt road we'd been looking for. I texted Leslie the location, and within ten minutes she showed up to rescue us.

The wind was predicted to be 10–15 miles an hour out of the southwest, and sixteen of our twenty miles today were heading southwest. But the wind never materialized. It never blew more than 5 miles an hour, and the slight headwind actually helped cool us off a bit. It did hit eighty degrees, but it was overcast for most of the day.

Dinner and beer at Zag's, outside of Mt. Vernon, Indiana. I'm exhausted.

Day 39 is now in the books. Six days to go.

DAY 40

October 26, 2024

Mile 847 to the Caseyville, KY, boat ramp

24 miles
Total: 871 miles

Towns and locks: Old Shawneetown (858)

Only 110 miles to go, and hopefully just five more days!

Five days still seems like a long time. Five days is longer than most people I know would ever go on a canoe trip. It will feel like we still have a long way to go until the afternoon of the last day, when we'll only have a few miles to get to the Ohio River's confluence with the Mississippi River. Paddling six or seven miles takes a fair amount of time and energy. Hell, even paddling a mile in a loaded solo canoe can take a while.

I woke up next to Leslie this morning in our one-star hotel in Mt. Vernon, Indiana. It's always nice to wake up next to Leslie.

Breakfast at our shithole hotel consisted of a dirty eating area with a small fridge that contained a gallon-size container of milk, maybe a quarter full; a half-full jug of SunnyD fake orange juice; a few old bagels; one packet of cream cheese; three plastic cereal bins, two of which were empty, the third full of a stale, generic version of Cheerios; slices of white bread for toast with no sign of any jelly or butter; several slightly bruised Red Delicious apples; and a mini-waffle maker.

After choking down a bowl of the off-brand cereal, I went straight to McDonald's for a Bacon, Egg & Cheese Biscuit and some mediocre coffee. VO, on the other hand, had one of everything at the hotel's nasty "breakfast buffet."

It was a half-hour drive back to the feed-corn field where Leslie had picked us up yesterday. She dropped us off, and VO and I walked back through the locked gate.

As we walked the half mile along the cornfield, six or seven gunshots rang out. They seemed awfully close. I could see it in my mind: Leslie driving away just as one of us got shot for trespassing.

Trespassing. A man protecting his private property from vagrants. A pretty solid defense. We picked up the pace.

It was a great relief to arrive back at our boats un-shot, and to see the boats were still where we'd left them, on an expansive sandy beach along the river.

The predicted 15-mile-an-hour wind from the north didn't kick in for the first mile. Then it shifted into high gear. We had shoved off around 8:15 this morning, and from 9–11:30, the wind was blowing 15–20 miles an hour but gusting higher, pushing us from behind. The waves quickly got up to two feet high, and we both fought for two and a half hours to keep our boats going as straight as possible and keep them from rolling over.

Big waves came from behind and rolled up underneath my flat-bottomed canoe, pushing my stern in one direction and the front of my boat in a different direction as the waves rolled up to the bow.

Wave after wave after wave.

Paddling closer to shore just meant the reverberating waves would bounce off the shore, causing a swirling mess of confused water. At certain points, it worked better to stop paddling and just hang on while I furiously steered using only my rudder pedals.

It was tense. Nerve-wracking. And I felt a lot of anxiety. As I told VO, I didn't feel scared, just tense and on edge.

The whole morning was like that.

We picked spots at mile 20 (Saline Landing) and mile 23 (an RV campground), both on the Indiana side, as possible places for Leslie to meet us, but we had been paddling on the Kentucky side all morning and there was no way I was going to attempt to get back across the river with these waves.

Around 11:30 a.m., we got to a boat ramp and sandy beach that was out of the wind and across the river from Old Shawneetown, Illinois. I called Leslie and told her there was likely going to be a change in plans and she'd have to pick us up on the Kentucky side of the river.

After a short break to calm my nerves, we ventured back out into the mayhem. Shortly after passing Old Shawneetown, we rounded a corner and started heading southwest, which blocked the north wind a bit. We still had a stout tailwind, but it wasn't quite as bad.

By 3 p.m., we'd paddled 24½ miles—in six hours and forty-five minutes—to a boat ramp in Caseyville, Kentucky, where Leslie was waiting for us.

More trees seem to be turning bright fall colors along both sides of the river today. It's already October 26. It seems like leaf colors should be over by now, but we *are* heading farther and farther south. Most of the leaves we saw were just turning brown and blowing off on windy days like today. But we did see some color.

The paddling from noon to 3 pm., the final 13 miles, was really pleasant. A manageable tailwind, sunny skies, and a temperature that barely hit seventy.

Getting 24½ miles in by 3:00 was a fantastic day for us. We had beer and dinner at the Half Moon Saloon in Mt. Vernon, Indiana.

It's hard to believe that today is Day 40 on the river. The Ohio River seems bigger now. Definitely wider. Some spots were up to a mile wide today. Crisscrossing from side to side may be a thing of the past.

The Wabash River joined the Ohio today, and that is no small river. In a couple of days, the Cumberland and Tennessee Rivers will also join the Ohio. So the river will continue to get bigger over the next few days.

And maybe, just maybe, it will start developing a little current? Probably too much to ask.

DAY 41

October 27, 2024

Caseyville, KY, boat ramp to the boat ramp at mile 897

26 miles
Total: 897 miles

Towns and locks: Cave-In-Rock (881), Elizabethtown (889), Rosiclare (892)

It's 5:55 p.m., and the sun just dropped below the horizon. It's getting cold very quickly. Two hours ago, I was sweating on the river and just now I put on long pants, my sweatshirt, a down coat, and my fleece hat.

Today was a perfect paddling day. Long, but the weather and the conditions were perfect. We left the hotel with Leslie at 7 a.m. and stopped at McDonald's for a large coffee with three shots of espresso. And three egg-and-sausage burritos.

It was an hour-and-ten-minute drive to get to the Caseyville, Kentucky, boat ramp where we had stopped yesterday. Then Leslie had to turn around and drive eight and a half hours back to Pittsburgh. So she was motivated to drop us off and get on the road.

The Caseyville boat ramp actually had a nice park and a few folks camping in trailers and tents for the weekend. If Leslie hadn't come to meet us, it would've provided a good camping spot.

We pushed off at 8:37 this morning and immediately paddled to the Illinois side, where we passed the Illinois-Indiana border on our right.

It was forty-two degrees when we jumped into our boats. I started out wearing long pants and a sweatshirt, but I had peeled my heavy layers off within an hour. No clouds. A very slight tailwind all day. Really nice paddling weather. It would've been great for a two- or three-hour paddle, but unfortunately, we needed to go at least 23 miles—with our second pull-out option at 26 miles.

After a few miles we paddled past the town of Cave-In-Rock, Illinois. There was also Cave in Rock Island, which featured the actual big cave in a rock wall: a massive hole in the side of a rock face along the river on the Illinois side. The cave had apparently been a hideout for river pirates who would attack passing paddlewheelers and other boats.

The town looked cute, but we didn't stop. At mile 14, we passed Hurricane Island, a big, four-and-a-half-mile–long island in the dead center of the river. At the far west end of the island was the little town of Elizabethtown, Illinois.

I found the Packers-Jaguars game on my SiriusXM phone app and listened to a great game that the Packers won 30–27 on a last-second field goal. That got me through a good two and a half hours of paddling.

We paddled past stunning fall colors and a handful of recreational boaters out enjoying a beautiful autumn Sunday. But otherwise, the river was quiet. Very rural. No industry at all.

We decided around mile 17 that we'd skip the boat ramp at Carrsville, Kentucky, and push on to the boat ramp at mile 26. There was wind and rain in the forecast through the rest of the week, so we wanted to get the miles in while we could.

Even after paddling 26 miles, we were done by 4 p.m. The concrete boat ramp was falling apart, like it hadn't been used in decades, and it didn't lead anywhere. The old gravel road was all grown over. Once we pulled off, I climbed out of my canoe and into shin-deep, slimy mud. It was a clay-mud mixture that stuck to the bottoms of my shoes.

We hauled our stuff up to a grassy section on the edge of a farmer's tilled field. There were no houses or barns in sight. Surely no one would see us or even care that we were here for the night.

I set up my camp chair and plopped down to put on dry shoes and socks, and immediately I heard—then saw—a side-by-side ATV speeding toward us.

It screeched to a stop, and a guy in head-to-toe camo jumped out, glaring at me. VO was still down by the river.

I gave him my best smile, then reached out my hand. "Hi, my name is Jon. My buddy and I are paddling the Ohio River, and today is Day 41."

The guy ignored my outstretched hand. "What's your last name, Jon?"

"Wunrow."

"Well, Jon Wunrow, this is private property. You need to leave."

"We were just hoping to spend the night. We'll be gone by 8 a.m. tomorrow."

"It's private property," he repeated. "I don't own it. I just drive around and keep an eye on things."

"In that case, could we ask the owner for permission to spend the night? We just paddled twenty-six miles to get here, and we're exhausted."

Just then, VO came up over the bank with his arms full of camping stuff. He saw the guy and stopped.

The guy threw his arms up. "What, are you guys moving in?"

We softened him up a little by talking about camping and canoeing, topics that clearly interested him. After twenty minutes or so, he introduced himself as Wes. Then he glanced around, lowered his voice, and told us we could stay.

"But," he said, "if the owner's daughter or nephew catches you, they're going to ask you to leave."

"Understood," I said. VO nodded.

"And don't mention you talked with me," Wes warned.

He hopped back into his ATV. "By the way, I have a river camp about half a mile farther down the river with a small grill and cooker out front. If you do get kicked out, you're welcome to camp there." He started the engine of his ATV, then turned back to us. "You really should be carrying a small rifle so you can shoot yourself a couple of squirrels. A man's gotta eat, no? Raccoon is good eatin', too. Ever had raccoon?"

"No, sir," I said, shaking my head. "I've never eaten raccoon. Have you, VO?"

To my surprise, VO hadn't either.

Wes drove off in his side-by-side. That was at 4:30 p.m. By 6:20, with no sign of a daughter or nephew, I figured we were okay.

I'm looking ahead to the next couple of days of paddling. It's hard not to think ahead. There's a tiny town at mile 23 tomorrow, across from where the Cumberland River drains into the Ohio: Hamletsburg, Illinois. So we'll shoot for that. Planning to paddle twenty or more miles each day still feels a little overwhelming, even though we've been doing it pretty much every single day of this trip.

It'll be chilly in the morning, so we'll just get up and do what we do every day: make some coffee, eat some oatmeal, and pack up.

Only four more days of paddling. Crazy!

DAY 42

October 28, 2024

Mile 897 to Hamletsburg, IL

24 miles
Total: 921 miles

Towns and locks: Golconda (903), Bay City (911), Birdsville (914½), Smithland Lock and Dam (918), Smithland (920), Hamletsburg (921)

We got out of our boats at 5:30 p.m. I had put in at 8:15 a.m. Almost nine hours on the river.

We sat for two hours at Smithland Lock and Dam at mile 21. It was the first time we'd had to wait to lock through since we'd been on the river. Once again, the small chamber was under construction, so only the big chamber was operating.

The wind started picking up around 11 a.m. Until then, we'd just had a slight headwind. But just before noon it started to blow a constant ten miles an hour, gusting higher. From then on, it was work.

While we were waiting to lock through, I called The Sand Bucket, a little bar along the river in Hamletsburg. The person who answered the phone, Lisa, told us we could camp down below the bar along the river. There was nothing else in Hamletsburg. Not even a post office. But there was this cute little riverside bar.

We had been trying to decide whether to paddle to Smithland on the Kentucky side of the river, where the Cumberland River drains into the Ohio, or stay on the Illinois side of the river and paddle two and a half miles farther to Hamletsburg—and The Sand Bucket. Smithland had a grocery store and not much else. And heading over there just to spend the night was a little out of the way.

When Lisa informed me that The Sand Bucket served pizza, the decision was made.

Today's paddle was beautiful. It was forty-two degrees when we got up. It felt colder than that to me, but it was super damp. Heavy dew covered our tents overnight, so we packed up some soaking-wet tents and rain flies.

When we got up this morning, we'd been in our sleeping bags for twelve hours. It was getting dark so early now. So by 6:45, I was ready to get up. It was a down jacket and fleece hat kind of morning.

The new MSR WindPro II stove I bought in Louisville—because my trusty MSR Reactor had finally crapped out—had been misbehaving. This morning it just shot out a plume of flame for five minutes before it eventually calmed down. I wasn't a big fan of this stove, especially after depending on my Reactor for hundreds of camping days on rivers and mountains around the world.

At the end of the day, we paddled up to a small, sandy beach, just below The Sand Bucket. Both of us were exhausted. It was almost 6 p.m., and the sun was setting as we unloaded our boats and hauled our gear several hundred yards to the nearest semi-flat spot for our tents. We set up our soaking-wet tents, then hiked uphill to the bar in the dark, with our journals and phone-charging cords.

We each had a couple of Blue Moons and an entire four-meat pizza. And I bought us a third pizza to go, for tomorrow's lunch.

Lisa the bartender had been fantastic, feeding us, letting us charge our devices, and keeping the beer coming. And one of the regulars, Rick, was super friendly too. It was so nice, after being in our boats for more than ten hours, to have an indoor place to eat and journal and unwind.

Rick turned to us. "Believe it or not," he said, "somebody saw an alligator in the river near here. And another thing. Up there around Cave-In-Rock, somebody said there were wild pigs. I'm not sure about that. Every year someone around here says they saw a black bear. I ain't never seen one, but I know they're around." Rick took his phone out to show us pictures of a giant deer, followed by all manner of local, animal-related photos.

Three more paddling days, if all goes well. Big winds are predicted for the next two days. We have exactly sixty miles to go!

As we left The Sand Bucket in the pitch dark, my headlamp picked up a Halloween display of a life-size skeleton puking into a bucket.

DAY 43

October 29, 2024

Hamletsburg, IL, to Paducah, KY

13 miles
Total: 934 miles

Towns and locks: Cumberland River convergence (922), Tennessee River convergence (932½), Paducah (934)

We woke up to wind. Trees swaying. Tent tarp fluttering. We had known the wind was coming, and here it was.

I wanted to get going right away, knowing it would be a long, slow day. So I started rustling around at 6:30 a.m. and was out of my tent and boiling water by 7, just as the horizon started glowing with morning light.

The tents had dried out overnight. I set my half of the third pizza toward the top of my day pack, knowing I'd be hungry by midmorning. Our goal was to paddle to Fort Massac State Park, just before the town of Metropolis, Illinois. That was the 23-mile mark, if the wind allowed us to make it that far. There was also a boat ramp around mile 15 on the Illinois side. And if we needed to pull off, Paducah was about 13 miles downriver on the Kentucky side. Paducah was where my cousin Jeff and I ended our Tennessee River thru-paddle in 2021.

There were several rock wing dams jutting out from the shore into the river. They help funnel water into the center of the river to create a bit of current for the big barges.

The wind was already blowing hard enough to create whitecaps, so I paddled close to shore where the water was a little bit calmer. For cover, I would paddle up behind each wing dam as I approached it, then paddle just to the edge of it and turn and paddle hard out around the wing dam and into the wind and waves.

It was very slow and hard paddling for about five miles. The river turned from heading due south and directly into the wind to more west-northwest, but as usual, the wind just followed the river and blasted us head on.

Between miles 5–9, we were able to get in behind some long, narrow islands, like Cottonwood Bar, so we were out of the direct wind for an hour. But by the time we paddled out from behind the final island, the wind had picked up and was slamming us broadside from the left. I'd been hoping we'd turned enough of a corner to get a push from the wind, but instead, waves built up as the wind pushed the water across the width of the river. And by the time the waves got to us on the right side, they were two feet high and bashing the left sides of our small boats. In a kayak, waves just broke over the bow and stern. It could be nerve-wracking, but there was no real fear of rolling over. But in a canoe, every wave risks pouring over the side and swamping me.

It was unnerving and exhausting trying to keep my canoe going relatively straight. I had to remain close to shore in case I tipped over, but far enough out that I wouldn't run aground. Meanwhile, the waves were constantly pushing me toward the shoreline.

After two miles of getting battered, we came up on several large rafts of barges tied together along the shore. Some were tied to large, concrete steel pylons out in the river, and others were tied off on the shore with massive cables. We paddled into some very narrow channels of calm water between the barges and the shore. Some of the channels were only a few feet wide. I had no interest in paddling around the outside of the barges in the wind and growing waves.

We were able to sneak inside the first three sets of barges, sometimes having to push large floating logs out of the way to get through. In between the sets of three or four tied-up barges, we'd have to paddle back out into the unprotected water and waves for several hundred yards before getting some shelter again for another short stretch.

At the fifth set of tied-off barges, the little channel between the barge raft and the shore was completely clogged with logs. After thinking about it for a few minutes, I agreed to paddle out into the chaos to go around them. We knew from a few days ago that the big waves crashing into the sides of the barges caused rebound waves in the opposite direction. So I paddled a good 150 yards out around the barges and well into the middle of the crazy river to try and avoid those rebound waves.

But 150 yards wasn't far enough away from the sides of the barges. Within seconds we were caught in massive waves coming from all directions. I was scared but calm. Several times I had to stop paddling just to get focused while being tossed in every direction, then paddle a few quick strokes in the direction I needed to head. My heart was in my throat.

We finally got around that long raft of several barges and paddled back behind the next set of barges, hoping to find a narrow channel along the shoreline. But it was tightly clogged with driftwood and logs.

We floated in the relatively calm water for fifteen minutes trying to decide what to do. The shoreline was too steep to pull our boats out, with cliffs as high as eighty feet.

We could literally see Paducah on the other side of the river, but the water was way too wild to attempt a crossing.

"I don't want to try paddling around any more barges," I finally said to VO. "It's too unsafe, and I feel like I'm pushing my luck." I could see several more barge rafts ahead, so we'd just have to keep doing this again and again.

"It would only take one wave to fill my boat," I continued, "and I don't want to be floating in the water and risk getting sucked underneath a massive barge." I'd already taken several small waves over the side and onto my lap. Not enough to capsize my boat, but enough to soak my shorts and shirt.

A few hundred yards back, we'd passed a small beach. We decided to paddle back to it, pull off the river, and contemplate our situation.

Once we were safely on shore, I pulled out my phone and looked at Google Maps. It showed that up above us, beyond the bluffs, were some farmers' fields, along with what looked like a dirt road about a mile away. The wind wasn't showing any signs of abating, and this small beach wasn't big enough to camp on. So we decided our best option was to haul our gear and boats up the steep bluffs to the field above, then decide if we were going to camp, leave our stuff and walk to the road, or another option that we hadn't thought of yet.

Then I remembered that two days ago, my paddling cousin Jeff had texted me the name and phone number of a local paddling enthusiast who lived in Paducah, Jeff Cantor. My cousin Jeff had stayed in contact with Jeff Cantor since we'd met him two years ago at the end of our thirty-five–day paddle of the Tennessee River in 2021. Jeff Cantor was part of the Tennessee RiverLine group that had provided us help and support during our Tennessee River thru-paddle. My cousin Jeff and I turned out to be the first thru-paddlers of the Tennessee River after RiverLine was created, so we became sort of the poster kids of their efforts. Cousin Jeff was sure that "Paducah Jeff" would find a way to help us out.

I'd met Paducah Jeff again a year later at the annual Tennessee RiverLine conference that was held in Alabama last year. I called Cousin Jeff to talk through our options, and he reached out to Paducah Jeff. Within forty-five minutes, Paducah Jeff had agreed to drive up as close to the farmer's field as he could get, pick us up along with our boats and gear, and bring us across the river to Paducah for the night.

"I'm three miles away as the crow flies," he had told us on the phone, "but it'll be a forty-five–minute drive to come get you."

With a plan in place, VO and I hauled all our gear and boats up the near-vertical bluffs, took a break and drank some water in the eighty-one–degree heat, carried a load of gear halfway to the dirt road, dropped our loads, then went back for our trailered boats and more gear for a second trip. It was exhausting work, especially after battling the river for most of the day. But we felt good about having a plan, and

I appreciated the physical movement. I don't sit still very well.

More high winds were forecast for tomorrow, and the next day wasn't looking much better: high wind followed by six hours of thunderstorms, then ten hours of rain. The thought of camping along the river for the next forty-eight to seventy-two hours in stormy weather was not appealing in the least. Especially being so close to the end of our trip.

As I was dragging my boat to where I'd dropped my first load, a side-by-side ATV came barreling toward me. The two young men inside stared me down.

They stopped and jumped out. "What are you guys doing here?" one of them barked.

Their initial hostility quickly turned into friendly conversation. Their names were Blake and Josh, and they ended up loading VO's kayak on the back of their ATV along with all our packs and gear. I sat on the back of the ATV and towed my trailered boat behind as they drove us the rest of the way to the dirt road we'd seen on the map. Nice!

Blake and Josh noticed the Harris-Walz bumper sticker on the side of my canoe.

"Do you mind if I ask why you like Harris?" Blake said.

"If I tell you the honest truth," I said, "do we still get a ride?"

We ended up having the best in-depth conversation about why I detested Trump and loved Kamala Harris. They shared their opinions as well. It was very civil and pretty cool.

Shortly after Blake and Josh took off, Paducah Jeff pulled up in his SUV. I totally recognized him from a couple of years ago. We loaded up our stuff. Jeff's double kayak rack held both of our boats perfectly. We didn't have any plans for where to spend the night in Paducah, so Jeff recommended a friend who owned the Belle Louise, a historic guest house. Owners Melinda and Cary, along with their son Colt, had completely restored this historic mansion. It was absolutely incredible.

After we met the owners, settled in, and took showers, we all went out to dinner at a restaurant called Over/Under with Jeff and his wife,

Teresa. Both amazing people who perfectly fit the definition of "river angels." After dinner and beers and great conversation, it was time for bed after a very, very long day—but not before enjoying a nip of complimentary bourbon in the parlor of the Belle Louise.

Before we went to sleep, we made a plan for the next couple of days, taking into account the predicted weather that was on the way.

DAY 44

October 30, 2024

Paducah, KY, to the River Road boat ramp

10 miles
Total: 944 miles

Towns and locks: Not much

Today was another poor-weather day. The winds were predicted to strengthen in the early afternoon, and we only had two options for places where Jeff Cantor could pick us up for a second night at the Belle Louise bed and breakfast.

We also know that with predictions of big storms, tomorrow will be a zero-mile day, which is why it looks like we'll be spending three nights in Paducah. We'll try to squeeze out as many miles as we can this morning before the weather turns bad and just take what the weather gives us.

Jeff has been terrific, willing to adjust his work schedule to help us out in any way he can.

After a delicious breakfast provided by Melinda, Jeff hauled us and our boats down to the Paducah boat ramp, almost directly across from where we had pulled off yesterday on the other side of the river. We were surprised to have just a touch of a tailwind, and by 11:30 a.m., we had already paddled ten miles out of Paducah to the River Road boat ramp on the Kentucky side. It was tough to stop so soon, but the next pickup option was twelve miles farther downriver, and the wind was already starting to pick up.

VO and I had planned to leave our boats and a few bags off in the woods next to the boat ramp. We'd already cable-locked them to a tree, but Jeff strongly encouraged us to throw everything on and in his truck so it wouldn't get taken or damaged overnight.

After a very relaxing afternoon of showers, naps, and some computer work, we met Cary, Melinda, Colt, Jeff, and Stacy at Stella's restaurant for a Smoked Old Fashioned, which Melinda said was the best old fashioned she'd ever had. And it was really good! We each had two drinks, then a nice dinner.

We had the best waitress at Stella's, who of course knew Melinda. Really funny and friendly. She claimed she could predict the weather by a bump on the back of her hand. I agreed to feel the bump, and she predicted bad weather for tomorrow.

I volunteered VO and me to pay for everyone's meals and drinks, to thank these folks for everything they had done to help us out. After I saw the bill, I apologized to VO for roping him into paying half, but it was worth it to be out with really nice people for the evening, talking about adventures and the river.

DAY 45

October 31, 2024

Paducah, KY

0 miles
Total: 944 miles

The wind and rain started around 10 a.m. and lasted pretty much all day and into the evening. Paddling and camping in this weather would have been miserable and maybe even impossible.

I'm only going to write about two things today:

1. Tonight is Halloween. Melinda and Cary are gone for the evening, so Melinda left us a basket of candy by the front door in case any trick-or-treaters come to the house. I just gave out candy to three cute little kids, which made me miss my grandkids and wish I were going house to house with them right now.
2. VO and I walked downtown to get dinner around 4:30. There are several cute restaurants and bars in downtown Paducah, especially on the main street. Since we'd already been to Over/Under and Stella's, we decided on Max's Brick Oven Cafe.

While we waited on the sidewalk for Max's to open at 5:00, we met the nicest older couple, Paula and Henry. Henry commented on my Green Bay Packers cap, and it turned out they were from just north of Madison, Wisconsin. They were in their late sixties (not so old, I guess) and were just coming back from spending a few months in Wisconsin, on their way to Boston to see a brand-new grandbaby.

We talked about our trip, and Henry, especially, was just amazed.

He couldn't believe what we were doing. He just couldn't fathom paddling 981 miles.

They were both so excited about our trip and were really encouraging. Henry said he had some health issues and was a big believer in taking risks and doing things while you still could. It lifted my spirits and gave me more motivation to paddle the last two days. VO and I sat near their table, out on the restaurant's side patio, and as we stood up to leave after dinner, Henry and Paula both got up to say goodbye and good luck.

"You guys are my heroes," Henry said.

That really touched me.

As we finished our dinner, I asked our waitress to put Paula and Henry's drinks on my bill, but not to tell them until we were gone.

I'm imagining their surprise and smiles right now.

DAY 46

November 1, 2024

River Road boat ramp to the Olmsted, IL, boat ramp

22 miles
Total: 966 miles

Towns and locks: Olmsted Lock and Dam (964½), Olmsted (965½)

It started to hit me today, on our last full day of paddling.

I imagined calling Leslie, Seth, Tyler, and my mom at the end of the river to say, "We did it!" And I got all choked up.

VO and I are sitting by an amazing campfire along the side of the river at mile 966. Mile 966 of the Ohio River! There were definitely days when this mile marker seemed a long, long way off.

We've been talking about the mental barriers. Fears. Excuses people give for never attempting a trip like this.

I know most people would never even want to do an adventure like this. I get that. But so many people I encounter say things like, "I would love to do what you're doing someday." But they will never, ever do it.

Why? What makes people say they really want to do something, then never even attempt it? The list of excuses is long.

Fear?

Job restrictions?

Poor health?

Lack of money, confidence, or support from their spouses or family?

The idea is too overwhelming?

It doesn't matter. I'm just curious.

All I know is that over the years, and even over the last couple of days, I've met people who have said, "I would love to be able to do what you're doing." So why don't they?

On the river, you think about wind a lot.

You think about weather.

You think about mileage and take-out points and where you're going to camp or sleep that night.

You think about how your shoulders ache, about how long it's been since you had your last Advil.

You think a lot about food.

And you think about seeing eagles, blue herons, and deer.

You think about the people that you love at home.

But not much else.

It's a simple life, paddling the river.

An uncomplicated life.

After tomorrow, the simple life will be gone again until my next adventure.

At the Belle this morning, Melinda was already knocking around at 5:00 getting breakfast ready. When we got up at 6:30, Cary was there, eager to have coffee with us before we headed out.

Jeff Cantor picked us up at 7:30. We loaded our boats and gear onto Jeff's SUV, and we were back at the River Road boat ramp by 8 a.m.

Jeff took a few photos of us as we paddled off on our last full day on the Ohio River. It was a chilly forty-four degrees with a five-mile-an-hour breeze out of the north-northeast, to our right. But otherwise, a cloudless, beautiful morning.

Twenty-two miles, even if it is the last full day of a forty-seven–day trip, is a long way to paddle. But it was a beautiful paddle, and I tried to keep my mind in a grateful space. Grateful to be on this amazing river. Grateful to be paddling it at sixty-three years old. Grateful to be very close to being done.

We stopped around mile 10 for a stretch and butt break. VO would've just kept on going if I hadn't suggested we stop. He's a machine.

We could see the final lock on the Ohio River, Olmsted Lock and Dam, over seven miles in the distance. It didn't bother me to see it so far away today, because this was our last full day on the river, and our last lock to paddle through. Olmsted is a relatively new lock and dam. It was under construction for decades but just completed two years ago. It's so new that it isn't even shown in our paddling map book.

We worried it might be the busiest lock on the Ohio, being so close to the Mississippi River, but we pretty much locked right through.

We have an amazing driftwood campfire right on the river tonight. My tent spot is a little uneven, but I'll just keep my head on the uphill side.

A perfect night to end our trip with. We finished off our bottle of Smith Holler whiskey that I bought in Cloverport, Kentucky, and are currently draining our bottle of Angel's Envy Finished Rye. No need to bring it home.

The one remaining dinner I have in my food bag is left over for a reason, so I'm about to have a peanut-butter-and-honey tortilla and a bowl of granola cereal for dinner.

VO is cooking up some nasty meal. I'm perfectly content with my tortilla, cereal, and whiskey.

It's 6:37 p.m., and the sun is long gone. The fire is blazing. The whiskey is setting in.

Perfect night.

Epilogue

That's where my Ohio River journal ended: "Perfect night." That was the night before we reached the spot where the Ohio and Mississippi Rivers converge.

Thinking back on it as I write this book, it seems fitting that the end of my journal was not reaching Fort Defiance State Park in Cairo, Illinois, where the Ohio River joins the Mighty Mississippi. Rather, my journal ended with a perfect night camping along the river's edge with fifteen more miles to go.

Maybe it's not the destination that matters after all. A lot of days, the thought of arriving at the 981st mile was what kept me going, picturing coming to the bit of land that sticks out with the Ohio flowing down from the north and the Mississippi coming in from the northwest. But getting to the end of a long river, or trail, or summit of a peak is definitely not the point of it all.

We paddled to Fort Defiance State Park on Day 47 of our trip. With only one full day off for bad weather, that was a long time to be waking up, packing up, and paddling day after day. Anyone who's done a half-day canoe trip or a five-day paddling trip in the Boundary Waters knows forty-seven days is a long damned time to paddle a canoe.

I think a lot about why. I've been thinking about it since my first long-distance adventure thru-hiking the 2,600-mile Pacific Crest Trail forty years ago. And after completing dozens of long-distance thru-hikes, thru-paddles, and bicycle trips, and reaching thirty-five country high points in the Western Hemisphere, I still don't have a good answer. My family and close friends have stopped asking. I guess I just like doing it.

As I put the finishing touches on this book in December 2025, I'm researching and planning a trip to paddle the first one thousand miles of the Missouri River starting in Western Montana in May 2026, and in February 2026, I hope to travel to four more Caribbean islands to hike to the country high points. I guess I just like doing it.

I love daydreaming, logistics planning, traveling to new places, meeting interesting people, feeling great when I accomplish a big goal, pushing my body and mind when they don't want to be pushed, seeing a sky full of stars at night, sitting by a driftwood campfire, seeing an eagle in the morning, hearing my paddle dip into the water, getting to the point on a trip when throwing my pack on my back feels normal—like my pack belongs there—and seeing the expression on people's faces when they ask, "You're doing *what*?"

As I think back a little over a year later, Day 47 on the Ohio River went something like this ...

Jeff Cantor and Stacy met us a few miles into the morning at a boat ramp near Mound City, Illinois. Jeff had said he'd really like to paddle the final nine or ten miles of the Ohio River with us. VO and I could see them up ahead on the right shore, waiting for us to show up. The first five miles for VO and I had gone by quickly, and I wanted to enjoy these last few thousand paddle strokes. And having Jeff with us would make it even more enjoyable.

Jeff jumped into his boat to meet us on the water as we got closer. He didn't want us to have to slow down and wait for him as we passed. The three of us paddled close together and talked about the river and Jeff's extensive volunteer work with the Tennessee RiverLine 652 folks. Getting both new and experienced paddlers out onto the water.

We paddled around and past several tugs and big rafts of barges. The last few miles of the Ohio River is a busy place with ports and industry and lots of barges. A couple of times, we had to stop paddling for a few minutes to see what the massive boats ahead of us were going to do.

And before we knew it, Fort Defiance State Park came into view on the right. And we could see the Mighty Mississippi River converging with the Ohio to form an even bigger river as it headed south to the Gulf of Mexico. It brought back lots of memories of a day four years ago, when Cousin Jeff and I paddled past this same park on our Mississippi River paddle.

As we neared the tip of the state park, VO and I stopped to drift a bit as we called Leslie and Val and our sons to tell them we'd finished. Jeff floated on ahead and took photos as we paddled those final few hundred yards. Stacy was standing on the shore to welcome us, and Val pulled up shortly after.

We both felt lots of joy—and lots of relief—to be done. I always experience some grief when I finish a long-distance adventure. I'm instantly thrust back into normal day-to-day life and have a few days of melancholy as I transition from one life to the other.

The end of our forty-seven–day adventure was not very dramatic. We pulled our boats out onto a slippery, clay-mud shore and unloaded our gear as we'd done so many times before, then lugged our bags, equipment, and boats up to the parking lot. Jeff took off with Stacy, and VO and I climbed into Val's waiting car.

And within a couple of hours, I was at the Paducah airport, transferring my boat and gear to a rental car to start my journey back to Pittsburgh where Leslie and I live, and where this whole thing began.

Packing List for the Ohio River

When packing for a multi-day paddling trip, think through the things you need to have within arm's reach while you paddle, taking different weather conditions into account.

For everything else, I use a series of waterproof dry bags organized by function. Capsizing is always possible, so I make sure everything can be submerged and remain dry.

Just remember, everything has to fit in your boat!

WEAR ON DAY 1

- Short-sleeved button-up shirt
- Shorts
- Undies
- Ball cap
- Sunglasses
- Paddle shoes
- Windbreaker

STRAPPED ONTO THE SPRAY DECK OR INSIDE MY BOAT

- Day bag
- Monkey Face (my paddling mascot)
- Portage wheels
- Bailer
- Life jacket
- Seat cushion (with back)
- Cable and lock
- 2 sets of paddles
- 2 water bottles

- Pee bottle
- Guidebook and map case
- Small notepad with pens (for daily notes)
- 4 carabiners
- 2 one-gallon water jugs
- Bilge pump
- 100-foot bow line
- 25-foot stern line

ACCESSIBLE DRY BAG DAY PACK

- Phone and waterproof case
- Phone charging cord
- Power bank and cord
- Wallet (credit card, cash, insurance card)
- Bug dope
- Sunscreen
- Advil
- Sunglasses and case
- Extra sunglasses and case
- Butt wipes
- Extra lighter
- Raincoat
- Windbreaker
- Wireless headphones
- AM/FM radio
- Lunch for Day 1

65-LITER DRY BAG

- Therm-a-Rest
- Tent (including poles, stakes, lines, ground cloth)
- Sleeping bag (in a dry bag)
- Pillow
- Clothes dry bag
- Small, collapsible table
- Camp chair
- Water filter

ELECTRONICS DRY BAG

- 2 power banks and cord (for phone)
- Laptop and charger
- Power bank and cord (for laptop)
- Waterproof case for books, journal, pens, and work stuff
- Book
- Journal and pens
- Headlamp
- Extra AAA batteries for headlamp
- Extra AA batteries for radio

CLOTHES DRY BAG

- Second pair of shorts
- 1 poly and 2 cotton short-sleeved shirts
- Long-sleeved button-up shirt
- Extra short-sleeved button-up shirt
- 3 pairs of underwear
- 2 pairs of boxers

- Pair of long pants
- Running/dry shoes
- 2 pairs of poly socks
- Lightweight camp shoes
- Rain pants
- Long-sleeved fleece shirt or sweatshirt
- Fleece jacket
- Warm hat and gloves

COOKING DUFFLE

- MSR Reactor stove
- MSR Reactor pots
- Frying pan
- 2 fuel canisters
- Cooking utensils
- Eating utensils, bowl, plate
- Whiskey cup
- Coffee mug
- Sharp knife
- 2 lighters
- Garbage bags
- Ziplock bags (quart and gallon)
- Tupperware container for leftovers

MISCELLANEOUS DRY BAG

- Duct tape
- Towel
- Repair kit
- Boat repair kit and tools

- First aid kit (antibiotic ointment, sunburn cream, After Bite, bandages, belly meds)
- Hygiene kit (eye drops, toothpaste, toothbrush, dental floss, Q-tips, soap, shampoo, vitamins, cholesterol meds)
- Extra CO_2 cartridge for inflatable life jacket

FOOD DRY BAG

- 7 dinners
- 7 breakfasts
- 7 lunches

About the Author

Author **Jonathan Wunrow** is the grateful grandparent of future adventurers Arlo, Rio, Coletta, and Lucy; parent of amazing sons Seth and Tyler; and husband of his *anam cara*, Leslie. Of much less importance, he is also a supporter of Ukraine, cabin builder, beer brewer, coffee roaster, grant writer, tribal advocate, Green Bay Packers fanatic, and a dreamer who occasionally finds time to plan and enjoy long-distance adventures around the world.

In addition to pursuing his passion for climbing most of the highest peaks in the Western Hemisphere, Wunrow has hiked the 2,650-mile Pacific Crest Trail; thru-paddled the Mississippi, Ohio, and Tennessee Rivers; bicycled across Mongolia; and climbed dozens of country high points, including Kilimanjaro with his son Seth. He and Leslie have also hiked the 870-mile Wales Coast Path, England's 630-mile Southwest Coast Path, and most recently, a 357-mile route across Ireland.

Wunrow has also authored *We are Nomads: A Bicycle Trip Across Mongolia* (2025), *A Walk Across Ireland* (2023), *Me and Sadie, We Got Everything We Need: Stories from Paddling the Tennessee River* (2022), *Paddling the Mississippi: One Story at a Time* (2022), *Never Stop Walking: A Wales Coast Path Adventure* (2021), *High Points: A Climber's Guide to South America* (2018), *Adventure Inward: A Risk Taker's Book of Quotes* (2013); and *High Points: A Climber's Guide to Central America* (2012).

Jonathan Wunrow's *Adventure Inward: A Risk Taker's Book of Quotes*

Extreme sports meet motivation and inspiration

Written for adventurers and non-adventurers alike, Jonathan Wunrow's collection of quotes and insights will inspire risk takers and thrill seekers of all sorts, encouraging personal exploration, offering guidance, and engaging in the ultimate adventure: inward.

Through his own experiences as an avid mountain climber, Wunrow (www.jonwunrow.com) and his work use quotes to explore the nature of why extreme sports enthusiasts do what they do, and how their risk-taking impacts them and those around them. The fifteen topics explored in *Adventure Inward* offer perspectives on life, death, purpose, and meaning, not just for risk takers and extreme sports enthusiasts, but for people of all walks of life.

Praise for *Adventure Inward: A Risk Taker's Book of Quotes*

Wunrow discusses why some take extreme risks, how it impacts on their lives and the lives of their loved ones, and how taking risks can make one feel truly alive ... it won't matter if you've never even been near a mountain or risked edging the speedometer of your car a mile or two over the speed limit. There are quotes in here that will speak directly to you ... [This book is] an inspirational call to live life fully. Settle in for a read, and listen to the voices collected in Adventure Inward: A Risk Taker's Book of Quotes. *They have a lot to say and it's all well worth hearing.*

—Jack Magnus, Readers' Favorite

Adventure Inward *consists of inspirational and humorous quotes designed to get readers thinking about their own course in life, and it reaches its own summit in tackling the bigger questions of life purpose. Even if you're not a natural risk-taker, it will provoke reflections on life's meaning that ultimately lead to transitions and changes ... and lest you think you need to be a sports enthusiast to properly absorb his adages, let it be said that the only prerequisite is an interest in self-growth and understanding life paths and transition points. If it's an inspirational and thought-provoking reader that's desired, packed with quotes and insights for personal advancement, then* Adventure Inward *more than fits the bill.*

—D. Donovan, eBook Reviewer, Midwest Book Review

A wonderful book. Adventure Inward *does a great job of explaining many existential issues concerning life, death, and one's purpose. I would definitely recommend this book to readers who like extreme sports and also to anyone interested in contemplating life's mysteries.*

—Avery Griffin, author of *The Demon Rolmar*

An excellent compilation of inspiring, humorous, and thought-provoking quotes sure to get anyone, no matter their hobbies, pastimes, or interests, thinking deeply about their world and what it means for us, as humans, to look inside ourselves. Each chapter is adorned with Wunrow's clear voice and unfailing insight into the human psyche in the presence of "risk" and the many ways this can be interpreted ... Wunrow has done a wonderful job writing and compiling this book. It will make an impression and spur you to thought.

—Bri Bruce, surfer and author of *The Weight of Snow*

I loved this book. It is surprisingly relevant to anyone's life. A good quote can inspire, transcend, counter negative thoughts, help us dream, allow us to escape, validate our thinking and beliefs, and offer basic truths. The quotes, proverbs, and sayings Jonathan Wunrow has collected from people of all kinds during his years of mountain climbing experience can translate to life itself.

—Amanda Mac, Something to Ponder About Book Reviews

Inspiring reading! Wunrow has written a wonderful gem for all those who appreciate, or want to better understand, the human urge to adventure. The author presents his own personal insights in uniquely themed chapters that are jam-packed with thought-provoking and funny quotations.

—Logan, Amazon customer review

www.ingramcontent.com/pod-product-compliance
Lightning Source LLC
LaVergne TN
LVHW010550110826
845149LV00003B/618

* 9 7 9 8 9 9 8 8 2 3 7 4 9 *